Salvation Through Slavery

Especially for Madeleine —
thank you for your years of
support and love while I was
writing this book.

Much love,
Henrietta

Salvation Through Slavery

Chiricahua Apaches and Priests on the Spanish Colonial Frontier

H. Henrietta Stockel

University of New Mexico Press ❧ Albuquerque

Library of Congress Cataloging-in-Publication Data

Stockel, H. Henrietta, 1938–
  Salvation through slavery : Chiricahua Apaches and priests
on the Spanish colonial frontier / H. Henrietta Stockel.
      p. cm.
  Includes bibliographical references and index.
  ISBN 978-0-8263-4325-3 (cloth : alk. paper)
1. Chiricahua Indians—Missions—Mexico.
2. Jesuits—Missions—Mexico—History.
3. Franciscans—Missions—Mexico—History.
4. Indians, Treatment of—Mexico—History.
5. Indian slaves—Mexico.
6. Christianity and culture—Mexico—History.
7. New Spain—History.
8. Mexico—History.
I. Title.
  E99.C68S764 2008
  972'.000497256—dc22
                    2007030132

Book design and type composition by Melissa Tandysh
    Composed in 11/14 Minion Pro ⟨⟩ Display type is Kinesis Std
    Printed on 60# House Natural Smooth B18 ⟨⟩

For Deshina, the Little White Girl in Cochise's Camp
and for
Madeleine H. Smith, as Promised

Contents

༄

List of Illustrations

✿

Acknowledgments

༽

My gratitude flows in rivers to the Chiricahua Apaches of New Mexico and Oklahoma who, during the last twenty-five years, have shared their history and lives with me; made me welcome and wanted; nourished my body, and especially my spirit; and applauded, questioned, and criticized my work. In contrast to Hollywood's and pulp fiction's portrayals of their ancestors, these descendants of the historical Chiricahua Apaches are a gentle people, tolerant, and unassuming. A justifiable wariness exists, though, a deeply suppressed caution that can occasionally be sensed at the edges of a pleasant greeting. It is not there in my case anymore, having dropped off somewhere in the late 1980s, but I cannot forget the feeling. The Chiricahuas who were youngsters back then are adults now with children of their own, and it is my privilege to hold in my arms their latest generation, heirs of those who survived the murder killers from three nations—Spain, Mexico, and the United States—have visited upon them.

The late Louise d'A. Fairchild was my *sine qua non* for more than twenty years. With her by my side or in the wings I was able to write several books about the Chiricahua Apaches with the freedom from worry that often plagues writers. She and I traveled together frequently through the years to the Mescalero Apache Reservation and to Apache, Oklahoma, where the Chiricahuas live now, so many times that I have lost count. She became part of that universe as much as I did, and the elder Apaches and I still weep at our loss. The young adults also miss their Weezie and recall with affection the good times they had with her for many years.

Madeleine H. Smith rescued me, threw me a life raft loaded with what I needed exactly when I needed it, and I caught it. I hung on for nearly three years.

Special friends must always be appreciated. Reverend Mother Marian Kelley, walking, talking, and traveling companion, listens well and advises even better, a true teacher. Catherine Ohrin-Greipp, a Cherokee woman who is not a wannabe and is as strong in her opinions as I am in mine, is a good match for me. Sally Dammery, an Australian, friend to the aborigines and recognized writer, has been my longtime daily communicator and commenter, thanks to e-mail. A special tip of the hat to Matt Babcock for all the research about Janos he compiled and copied for me at the University of Texas, Austin. Lois and John McQuaid helped me understand and appreciate the limits of Christianity, a complex topic not for sissies to explore.

Three of the men in my life enrich it. Siggy Jumper, a Chiricahua Apache/Seminole from Florida, brought his family history to my table, and I continue to listen in awe and with respect as he unfolds it. John Rose, colleague, collector *extraordinaire*, and expert on Tombstone, lives nearby and does not hesitate to share his wide-ranging knowledge about the American West and its peoples with me. Wesley Billingslea, head of the Family Teotl, full of energy and enthusiasm, impresses me with his unbounded reverence for the lifeways and struggles of the peoples of the lost cultures.

Last, my blood. Lorrie and Selah Stone bring unconditional love and the future into my life. My dearest hope is that they will always look upon my work with pride. Brother and sister Erik and Erika Matousek remain close in my thoughts.

H. Henrietta Stockel
Sierra Vista, Arizona

Introduction

ᛒ IDENTITY THEFT IS ONE OF THE HOTTEST TOPICS IN THE EARLY years of the twenty-first century, but it is not new to the millions of descendants of indigenous peoples who confronted colonizing Europeans, especially the clergy, on northern Mexico's Spanish colonial frontier.¹ Identity theft was then called baptism, a religious sacrament Roman Catholic missionaries introduced about 150 years after Columbus reached Hispaniola's shore. Baptism and renaming were the first step in imposing a new way of life on the indigenes for which there were no words in their ancestral language.

Imposing new names on someone or something that already has a name is an excellent example of Eurocentrism—the notion of cultural supremacy the Spaniards brought with them into northern Mexico. It is one of the main topics of this book. From the Indian point of view the outsiders exhibited impressive daring and courage by disrespecting and eradicating names that had been theirs since the beginning of their lives and were, in many cases, considered sacred. As a consequence of their utter disregard the newcomers assumed a larger-than-life stature, for in the eyes of the preliterate peoples, no one but a god would act so audaciously. Identity theft through baptism, then, wrapped the Spaniards in an aura of mystery and authority, enabling them to capitalize on their efforts to colonize.

This painful drama began in the time before time when migrating forebears of the Chiricahua Apaches allegedly crossed the Bering Strait from west to east. Not everyone agrees with this theory, however; at least one noted scholar and researcher openly challenged this conclusion. The late Vine Deloria Jr. asserted, "Nobody really knows. Almost every articulation of the Bering Strait theory is woefully deficient in proving a motive for the movement . . . In order to move Paleo-Indians across the Bering Strait, we must have the water level of the ocean drop significantly."[2] Deloria clearly referred to walking across the divide, as have others who support the low water/high water premise. There is another possibility, however. Through innate common sense and by making good use of their environment, including the washed-up debris on the shore, the adventurers could have constructed various conveyances to sail across the water. Regardless of how they did it, they got to the opposite shore, for linguistic evidence, one of the primary proofs, reveals that the language of these venturing natives, then called Athapaskans, is distantly related to Eyak, spoken on the north coast of Alaska.[3]

Once on the eastern shore, they continued to the McKenzie River valley, in the region of the Arctic Circle. They halted there and lived apparently for centuries, possibly until about the 1400s when, for unknown reasons, they began a migration southward that ended in northern Mexico, the area that became the Spanish colonial frontier, the Pimería Alta, and ultimately the American Southwest.[4] As one of history's coincidences, in far-off Europe, the same century produced an Italian sailor whose voyage would presage unadulterated misery for most Indian peoples on the North American continent.

Columbus's foot, pressed into the soft beach sands of Haiti and the Dominican Republic, signaled the beginning of European imperialism, a devastating process that dispossessed, displaced, or killed most of the indigenes, from the Caribbean Tainos in the late 1400s to the Southwest tribes four hundred years later.[5] Those few native inhabitants who psychologically succumbed to the newcomers but physically survived—a paradox—watched as the insolent authority the incoming Spaniards assumed replaced their territorial boundaries, political systems, ancient customs, and spiritual beliefs. The high tide of strangers—religious and military men, explorers, caravaners, farmers, settlers, merchants, miners, scammers, pillagers, vagabonds, rapists, ranchers, entrepreneurs, crooks, families, and adventurers from every walk of life—overwhelmed the Indians with their bodies, their diseases, their egos, their cultures, and their names.

Before contact with the Europeans, indigenous peoples had, for generations, made their homes in Mexico's high desert among abundant game, edible roots and seeds, plant medicines, venomous creatures, stubby trees, and low, thorny cacti. They relied on a continuing flow of cold water in streams and rivers and had grown accustomed to seeking shelter from the heat in the high, cool forests of massive mountain ranges. The Spaniards created a revolution in land use by defiling the environment—chopping down trees, killing wildlife, uprooting medicinal plants to grow Old World crops, building ranches and farms, and, significantly, erecting mission complexes atop the tribes' sacred sites. They dug arroyos to divert river water from its natural route through Indian villages and cut roads through pristine desert surroundings. They usurped Indian homelands and erected fences that limited access to sacred sites. New, powerful, negative emotions like disrespect and humiliation emerged in the psyches of the Indians and, confused and fearful, they no doubt turned to their cultures' traditional religious practices to understand the situation. Often, though, there were no words or ancient ceremonies to understand what was happening.

The Chiricahua Apaches, one of a number of indigenous groups living in the region when the Spaniards arrived, likely conducted spiritual rituals that asked for an explanation, praised Ussen, the Giver of Life, and reaffirmed their inferiority to their creator.[6] In their spiritual humility, the Chiricahuas believed that Ussen created them last, after he had finished everything else, and expected them to have a respectful, dependent relationship with their surroundings, divine instructions that were impossible to follow in the face of the destruction the Spaniards caused.[7]

The Christian Europeans on the frontier also honored their religious traditions, in particular the Bible, and called upon the holy book for guidance. In Genesis believers are given dominion "over all the earth," an idea that could be literally and figuratively interpreted to mean superiority over everyone and everything else.[8] With this sanctified background and the conviction they were following Christ's teachings, the Jesuit and Franciscan missionaries assigned to northern Mexico were determined to convert the native peoples into Christians and tax-paying citizens of the empire. To accomplish their goal, these clergymen believed they had divine permission to use every means at their disposal.

The two differing concepts—spiritual humble-heartedness versus biblical permission coupled with the egocentricity of empire—are responsible for much of the monumental collision between the European priests and the frontier Indians, Chiricahua Apaches included. One consequence of these dramatically opposing principles was identity theft through baptism, which preceded an even more destructive activity: enslavement.

The new information in this book is a sample of the unknown number of baptized Chiricahua Apaches the missionaries sold into slavery. Where possible, I will identify the priests who baptized them, bestowed the new names, and sold them, whether the clergy managed the transaction directly or indirectly through their Indian allies. When available, I will include the names of the purchasers, often identified in the records as "godfather."[9] Identity theft through baptism and the unconscionable act of selling human beings combine to form the core of this book.

Readers must understand that I do not speak for the Chiricahua Apaches, nor am I able to correctly and accurately interpret the full impact of the events the imperious Europeans forced onto the Chiricahua Apache people and culture. I agree totally with American Indian authors Clara Sue Kidwell, Homer Noley, and George E. Tinker who recognize that "Western categories do not work for identifying and describing, naming, or explaining Indian . . . realities."[10] I have learned through my long relationship with the Chiricahua Apaches that most academic frames of reference fail to address the range of contemporary Indian life and historic heritage. Still, in the past many indigenous peoples were reluctant to write their story. That is changing now. A few Chiricahuas are now beginning to speak for themselves, publicly and in writing, challenging educated white academicians who have written about the people from points of view that may have been inappropriate and inadequate. Until Chiricahua authors are published, however, non-Apache writers will continue to depict the events, as I have done now and in the past, that had an impact upon this rich culture.

This book, not an academic treatise by any means, is meant to appeal to a cross section of readers. I hope the material we authors present from our points of view will be acceptable to the Indian people we portray and receive their blessing.

The first chapter discusses the Chiricahua Apaches and gives readers an inside look at certain aspects of their culture. After that, a description of missions and missionaries will reveal the practical goals the colonial Jesuits and Franciscans set in the service of cross and crown. Then the spotlight narrows onto four sites—the presidio of Tubac, the missions of Tumacácori and Janos, and the country of Cuba. Tubac and Tumacácori, located just three miles apart, cooperated closely with each other and were, in some ways, interchangeable during the occupation. The following chapter is the heart of the book and highlights the Hispanicized names of a sample of the large number of Apaches who were sold into slavery in order to "save their souls." The final chapter presents a paradox: if the profits realized through selling human beings to save their souls were discontinued, the missions could not continue to fulfill their religious responsibilities to save souls and thus would fail to meet their purpose and sworn obligations.

A few caveats regarding my use of terms are appropriate. "Apache(s)" means only the Chiricahua Apaches. When other groups are referenced, I will us their full name, for example, White Mountain Apaches or Nednhi Apaches. My references to "Spanish priests" or "Spanish missionaries" are not literal in that many clergy on the colonial frontier were from other European backgrounds. "Pimas" should be understood to comprise members from the Pima, Pápago, and Sobaípuri tribes. It is helpful to remember that the American Southwest did not exist during the time of the Spanish colonial frontier; the area that is now southeastern Arizona and southwestern New Mexico was then part of Mexico. Consequently, my use of the terms "American Southwest" or "Southwest" is limited. Most of that area was known as the Pimería Alta, or Sonora, Mexico, and I use those designations often. Finally, the native peoples always thought of themselves in terms of the traditional names of their specific tribes until the forced "benefits" of cooperation with the Spaniards caused amnesia that has lasted until the current day; many Chiricahua Apaches have lost their tribal names forever.

Necessary to a full understanding and appreciation of the events described in this book is acceptance of the fact that, to the occupying Spaniards in the seventeenth century, the frontier and its inhabitants were theirs for the taking, regardless of the Indians' history or spiritual relationship with the land. The monumental collision of peoples and cultures was inevitable.

༃

CHAPTER 1

The Chiricahua Apaches

༃ ORAL TESTIMONY IS ONE OF THE OLDEST FORMS OF REPRODUCING history. Among contemporary Chiricahua Apaches oral testimony in the form of oral history, and oral tradition supports the claim of ancestral life in a cold climate, probably the areas of the Yukon and Northwest Territories. Claire Farrer recorded an Apachean myth that tells, "We were made in a land of Ever Winter" and describes "a House of Ice and Winter . . . on the shores of a big lake . . . Water that You Cannot See over . . . That land being The Land of, The Home of, Winter and the Home of Ice."[1] In interviews with a Mescalero Apache medicine man, the late Bernard Second, she also reported a reference to "when we were still in the North Country" as part of a creation myth he related to her.[2]

As further evidence of the people's presence below the Arctic Circle, Julia Cruikshank notes that in the far distant past, trade between the Tlingit and the Apaches' Athapaskan ancestors long existed around the Yukon and that "Athapaskan peoples [as they were then called] incorporated Tlingit themes into their storytelling traditions."[3]

These words do not explain why the Athapaskans initially left their home somewhere in Asia, probably Mongolia, to settle in cold country just south of the Arctic Circle. Their purpose may always remain a mystery. Clifford Coppersmith noted that "scant evidence exists that can more completely define the paths . . . as these hunter-gatherers left little behind to mark their passage."[4] Were they just wandering, or did they have a plan? Questions like these may never be answered in full, but it is plausible that some of these adventurers sailed across the Bering Strait previously, perhaps in search of food such as the caribou. The allure of successful hunts over a period of time could have set the entire movement in motion, relocating the people close to a more available and reliable food source.

The Athapaskans' second migration, this one southward from the Arctic Circle sometime during the late 1300s or early 1400s, is of major interest to this book. Richard Perry placed their arrival later, writing

> Apacheans arrived in the southwest core area within a few decades of 1500 A.D. [by] an irregular movement of small groups down along both sides and through the Rocky Mountains, with some entering the southwest by way of the Colorado Plateau, others along the eastern slopes and into the Sangre de Cristo Range and through the mountain chain itself. Most remained in or near mountainous areas."[5]

Kieran McCarty, OFM, a recognized expert on the history of the Franciscan presence in colonial New Spain, believed Perry's dates were too late. "It was about 1150 that the Apaches were traveling. They got down to around the Dakotas and tried to stop there, but the Sioux beat them back into the Rockies, so they kept moving southward. Then I also heard it was about 1125. Sometimes, though, the sources don't know from shinola."[6]

Jack Forbes's research supported one of McCarty's conclusions by claiming there were at least two mass migrations out of northern Canada by the Athapaskans, one group arriving in New Mexico in the 1200s or 1300s and driven out by the Pueblo Indians. This is hard to believe if one is familiar with the personalities of the groups, the friendly, accommodating Puebloans as opposed to the feisty, confident Chiricahua Apaches. Another group, different from Forbes's first reference, was in Arizona in the 1400s and could have been among the tribes that forced the abandonment of an important Mexican trading center known as Casas Grandes.[7] This sounds more like typical Apache behavior when their homelands were threatened or invaded.

Losing sight of them as they traveled southward is a disadvantage to historians. Without substantive oral or written information describing the migration, it is as if the Athapaskans suddenly popped up on the Spanish colonial frontier in the fifteenth century or later. Unfortunately, I could find nothing that supports my conclusion that these travelers undoubtedly met other indigenous groups along the way, for example, the Great Plains and Southern Plains tribes and New Mexico's Pueblo peoples. If I am correct, and if the Athapaskans were lucky, friendly Indians along the way extended invitations to join them, perhaps in winter when foot travel was difficult and hospitality most welcome. During these long months as guests, tribal customs were undoubtedly demonstrated, perhaps mutually exchanged and adopted, babies were born, elders died, personal alliances made. As the weather lifted and the journey restarted, some Athapaskans possibly stayed behind, and some of the host tribal members could have agreed to accompany their new friends. This same situation might have occurred over and over again with various new groups met on the long trek, so that when they finally reached northern Mexico, the adventurers were no longer strictly Athapaskans; the admixture of peoples and customs had modified their culture.

Gary Clayton Anderson defined this melding as ethnogenesis and reinvention, as indigenes altered themselves "culturally to forge unity with other groups, abandoning languages, social practices, and even economic processes to meet the needs of the new order."[8] This extreme is not necessary to accomplish a blending of sorts; combining selected customs in a syncretic relationship that benefited all parties could involve degrees of accommodation, rather than total abandonment, of customs and conventions.

Outside indigenous volunteers into the Chiricahua Apache life-style probably listened, when allowed, to stories that passed on the tribe's heritage through favorite legends. Legends communicate and explain things; they satisfy and interpret. They do not have to be logical, and they do not have to be similar. For example, in most traditional cultures, time-honored creation myths do not necessarily coincide with any anthropological, geological, archeological, or historical data; that is unnecessary since legends do not require evidence as proof. They just live in the hearts and minds of a people and are testimony to the enduring power of language to mold and shape belief. Like every culture's customs, Chiricahua Apache creation stories satisfactorily define major events to the people.[9]

Particularly important was the firm belief that their god, whom they called Ussen, was guiding their destiny and wanted them to stop migrating when they reached northern Mexico. Generations later, the great warrior Cochise affirmed his ancestors' earlier decision, noting, "I came here because God told me to do so."[10]

Other important figures talked about in Chiricahua legends such as White Painted Woman and her son Child of the Water do not, under any circumstances, compete with Ussen, the Giver of Life, the one acknowledged to be all powerful and to whom all honor and reverence as the ultimate deity is given. Ussen alone is thought of as the creator, the maker of world and man, and the source of all supernatural power.

In Chiricahua prehistory Ussen sent rain and a flood to wash away evil on earth. When the rain stopped, Child of the Water and White Painted Woman were alive and molded human beings to keep them company, thus creating the Apache people. Another story about a flood tells of only one mountain that was not entirely covered by flood water. Child of the Water was atop this mountain and made human beings—Apaches—from mud after the water subsided.[11] The concept of a flood appears in the stories of many ancient cultures and is not unique to Christianity.

Eve Ball recorded Warm Springs Chiricahua Apache James Kaywaykla's recollections of certain stories about the adored icon, White Painted Woman. "She was a woman of beauty and chastity," he said. "All men admired her but she refused to marry. A prolonged drought brought on a famine and many perished of hunger. As long as she had food she shared it. But a time came when without the miracle of rain nobody could survive. [A prior legend told of] a virgin willing to sacrifice her life to save the people. White Painted Woman decided to make that sacrifice. She went from her people and lay upon a rock awaiting death. In the night rain fell upon her and a child was conceived. Because he had no earthly father, people called him Child of the Waters, for he was the son of Ussen . . . All agree that this child was sacred. White Painted Woman had constantly to protect him from the attempts that sought his death. She dug a secret place and built a fire over the entrance. When danger threatened she hid the child in this cave. When it was safe she let him out to exercise."[12] The icons of White Painted Woman and Child of the Water hold places as exalted in the Chiricahua Apache traditional religion as do the Virgin Mary and Jesus Christ in Christianity. Their similarity is unmistakable.

Migrating Apaches carried these and other stories in words and songs from the north country to the Southwest desert. While the old legends remained constant in their hearts and minds, the people's arrival in the quite different arid environment caused cultural changes that became the stuff of the tribe's future stories. In other words, they were creating legends as they migrated and settled in northern Mexico.

For example, back up in the north country, animal hides served two major purposes, shelter and warmth. On the colonial frontier, while shelters could still be constructed of hides, a cooler, more appropriate lodge called a wickiup was a practical choice in the desert climate. Erected by women, a wickiup required carefully selecting branches from trees or tall shrubs. After plotting a circle, the women set the limbs into holes they dug in the ground a few feet apart. They pulled the leafy tops together and securely fashioned them with yucca leaf strands. When completed, this framework could be as high as seven feet in the center and as wide as eight feet around. The branches were covered with long native grasses, ocotillo stalks, boughs, or hides. An opening at the top center allowed smoke from a central indoor fireplace to escape. In rainy weather this smoke hole could be covered over with hides that were also used to protect the doorways. The interior dirt floor of the wickiup was lined with brush and grass that could be removed and replaced when dried out or when the woman swept the earthen floor with a broom made of grasses or leafy branches. For sleeping, robes made of hides were spread over the floor. The multiple uses of hides and the conical shape of the wickiup—resembling an igloo in form—perhaps reflected memories from the Arctic Circle.

As the latest indigenous group to arrive in the region, "the new kid on the block" was carefully observed by the neighboring tribes. (Here too valuable specific documentation is missing, so informed speculation is the best we can do.) Other Indians would have slowly and cautiously interacted with them, sized them up so to speak, until trust developed. Certainly clashes occurred, most probably in times of drought when intense competition limited further the decreasing supply of animal foods, edible roots and grasses, medicinal plants, and water.

In more normal times, the indigenes on the frontier did not consider the earth a commodity to be exploited, something that could be "owned," such as a piece of clothing. Tribes collectively enjoyed the land; it provided sustenance and was revered. The earth was holy and spiritual, made sacred by naming the locations. It was a place of power, of spiritual transformation, of wisdom. For some, it is still that way today. "The land makes people live right. The land looks after us," said White Mountain Apache Annie Peaches in 1978.[13]

To fully appreciate the deep regard for the land that many indigenous groups felt, it is necessary to believe that the sacred ancestral past was then and is still embedded in the canyons, arroyos, mountains, and fields. The land holds the life and death of loved ones, of relatives, extended families, friends, and children. To the newcomer Chiricahua Apaches, the land provided a place to pray, heal, and teach; a place where foods, medicines, and shelter offered life-giving support; a place to hide, a place to sleep, *the* place Ussen had selected for them. Listen to Kidwell, Noley, and Tinker discuss the relationship.

> Unlike nomadic European settlers whose impulse to explore drove men across the Atlantic in their search for wealth, Indian traditions tell of . . . homelands that were designated for them. Indian communities have an attachment . . . to particular lands, and our cultural identity is heavily invested in that attachment. It helps define the limits of our ceremonial life, to give a foundation to our traditional stories and myths, to secure a sense of balance and harmony in community identity . . . The sense of a spiritual association with the land . . . gives land a special place in the Indian sense of identity.[14]

Not to be overlooked is the moral significance of the frontier to the Indians. David Carmichael and his colleagues stated that the land "carries with it a whole range of rules and regulations regarding the people's behaviour in relation to it, and implies a set of beliefs to do with the non-empirical world."[15] These guides may be transferred to subsequent generations in stories and songs as parameters for social interactions, positive and negative. For example, humorous coyote tales can tell of the rascal getting into mischief and racing across the landscape, only to fall head first into a hole and disappear as payment for his bad deed. The meaning is clear.

Throughout history, the Chiricahua Apaches have perceived the land as connected with the creator of life, Ussen. That view remained, from its inception during the time before time well into the future when the famous Apache chief, Cochise, said, "I came here [to the southwest] because God told me to do so . . . God spoke to my thought and told me to come in here and be at peace with all."[16] For Cochise, Mexico and the American Southwest were not of his choosing. Instead, he believed it was selected for him by God, who revealed himself to Cochise, thus powerfully joining the two—God and Cochise—by means of the land. In the 1950s, Asa Daklugie, son of Chief Juh of Mexico's Nednhi Apaches, brought that same thought into the present, telling Ball, "He put the Apache on the land which he had created for us, and he laid down certain laws which we were to obey."[17] More recently, the comment of the late Chiricahua Apache leader, Berle Kanseah, regarding his tribe's homelands was similar: "It's ours, and it's sacred and it's how we were intended to be, placed here in the southwest."[18]

To the Chiricahua Apaches there is no doubt that the Creator selected the site that would become their home. Through this process he spiritually and physically anchored the people and their culture in the high desert hills, mountains, valleys, rivers, trees, and stones of the Southwest and northern Mexico. The entire region, known also as the Pimería Alta, was sacred to the Apaches as the personal manifestation of their creator's wishes, omniscience, and omnipresence.[19]

The Apaches developed a variety of techniques using most elements in the new environment to their best advantage. For example, northern Mexico's medicinal plants were initially unfamiliar, and their healing properties were different from the remedies the people had left behind. After a period of experimentation, the Apaches undoubtedly learned, identified, memorized, and then came to rely on certain of the local flora to cure their minor ailments.

Medicine women, who did most of the hands-on healing of minor problems, also took care of the bumps, bruises, and cuts inherent in high desert living. Moving about only on foot before contact with horses, the Apaches were always challenged by thorny cacti, falling rocks, varmint bites, and confrontations with wild animals. Creating a *materia medica* to address all the possibilities would have taken a considerable amount of a healer's time and energy and added immeasurably to her existing family obligations, but it was necessary.

Some medicines doubled as foods. The pods from the freely growing mescal bush, for example, were delicious when roasted and were also efficient at controlling bleeding from wounds. Chewing softened a raw mescal shell, and when there was nothing but the woody fibers remaining, a healer spit them out, rolled them into a ball, and plugged the wound. When hemorrhaging ceased, she removed the plug and inserted more chewed mescal deeply into the path of the wound. Over and over again she chewed and inserted until the wound was under her control, and the individual was able to continue on.

If a broken bone had to be set, an Apache medicine woman created a splint from sotol cactus slats, and, after immobilization, the bone and slats were wrapped with hide strips cut from the skin of once-living wildlife. To treat mundane maladies, she smashed one variety of the mesquite plant and placed it directly on scrapes, scratches, and some bug bites. The plant's beans could be ground into meal for food, and drinking a solution made from mesquite roots boiled in water was the treatment of choice for nervousness and colic; a fluid from the leaves served as an eyewash. The inner bark of the mesquite bush was so soft that it served as diapers for babies in cradleboards.

When more serious afflictions occurred, such as those from contact with snakes, giant scorpions, centipedes and other venomous desert dwellers, a medicine woman treated the wound first by killing the offending creature and then carving out a piece of its body to apply directly on the bite. The next best medicine was placing live crickets, lizards, and spiders on the injury. Routine aches and pains at the campsite or when traveling were helped by drinking a tea made from snakebroom—a prolific, many-stemmed plant with yellow flower clusters that grew almost everywhere on the new frontier. For a sore mouth, possibly the result of chewing berries, women squeezed juice from leaves and stems of the milkweed plant and mixed the liquid with secretions from pine and cottonwood trees to make a mouth-soothing chewing gum. Wild mint steeped in water eased a sore throat that might have resulted from yelling. To reduce fever, possibly from an infected cut, women boiled willow and quaking aspen leaves in water and offered it as a tea.[20] All these treatments were in place before the Europeans arrived and contemptuously imposed their own ideas of civilization, including Spanish medical remedies, on the indigenes. Without considerable effort that they did not expend, the newcomers could not know the power of Apache healing, particularly that involving the medicine men.

Apache medicine men were "in the zenith of their glory [when someone is taken sick]," wrote Bourke.

> Where there is only one person sick, the exercises consist of singing and drumming exclusively, but dancing is added in all cases when an epidemic is raging in the tribe . . . Prayers are recited . . . but very frequently the words are ejaculatory and confined to such expression as "*ugashe*" (go away), and again there is to be noted the same mumbling of incoherent phrases which has been the stock in trade of medicine men in all ages and places. Their use of gibberish was admitted by the medicine men who claimed that the words employed and known only to themselves (each individual seemed to have his own vocabulary) were mysteriously effective in dispelling sickness of any kind.[21]

Medicine men occupied an exalted position in the tribe. Good health and the means to achieve or recover it were always essential if the tribe was to survive as an entity. If someone, particularly an adult male, was ailing, the group's unending need for protection and hunt for food would be adversely affected by losing even one hunter in the small party. Relying primarily on a high protein and high fat diet, wild game and small animals were the single source of meat, coupled with plant foods and other natural nourishment such as honey, which young boys showing off their courage carefully gathered directly from hives. All duties in the encampment were clearly delineated. Men were warriors, raiders, and traveling hunters who sought mainly deer and elk, while boys shot at rabbits, squirrels, desert rats, and gophers in the immediate area. The women and girls blended the raw honey with crushed seeds to make a type of bread-paste. They harvested plants and herbs and butchered the large animals, cooked or dried the meat, gathered seeds, and also tanned the hides for clothing and protection against inclement weather. In their spare time, the women were also weavers, creating baskets from vines and other plant materials.

For people who many times moved encampments either out of necessity to avoid encounters with enemies or voluntarily to follow the seasons or the animals, crafting pottery was out of the question. Baskets were able to stand up to the stress of travel, did not break, and were lighter in weight than pots. Weaving also connected the women to the earth and through that affiliation to Ussen, so basketry became another way to praise the creator and express gratitude.

There are many meanings attached to the craft. Contemporary Apache basketweaver Tu Moonwalker said, "Basketry teaches you to be harmonious with yourself—because once you start the stitchwork, you find yourself doing it in a rhythm, a natural rhythm that belongs solely to you . . . It's sort of like self-hypnosis." She speaks with authority when she describes the wild flowers her grandmother used as dye and the way the older women worked with the materials. "The whole process of gathering had a ceremony, no matter what you were using. There are proper ways to be observed in the preparation of the materials . . . because with basketmaking, you really have to feel the whole connection in your soul." [22] No doubt this description reflects many of the same feelings historical Apache women held as they created baskets from the natural materials available in the new environment.

The cattail tule was a desert plant that provided pollen for use in ceremonies. Tule pollen, called *hoddentin*, has become one of the most sacred items in the Apache religion. To prepare hoddentin for ceremonial purposes, medicine men harvested the cattail plant from ponds and marshes when it was at a certain level of maturity. Back at camp they spread the bundle of collected tules onto a hide and let them dry in the sun. Next, they scraped off the brown covering and allowed the sacred yellow interior to fall onto the hide, where it continued to dry to a certain consistency before being gathered up and stored. Through prayers and incantations at each step of the drying process, the pollen was blessed and saved for later use.

Bourke reported a conversation with an Apache in the late 1800s about a particular use of hoddentin, but whether the examples provided reflected its use during the Spanish colonial frontier period is unknown.

The man told him, "When we Apache go on the warpath, hunt, or plant, we always throw a pinch of *hoddentin* to the sun, saying 'with the favor of the sun, or permission of the sun, I am going out . . . and I want the sun to help me.'"[23]

Bourke also recorded other uses of the tule, writing, "[It] is thrown to the sun in the early morning, is cast upon the trail of snakes, fills the air in war dances of unusual solemnity, and is used most freely [in prayer] around the couch of the dying."[24]

Each warrior leaving camp for a battle placed a pouch full of hoddentin somewhere on his person, often tucked into his ammunition belt, thus guaranteeing protection and success. Before mounting his horse, the fighter took a pinch of hoddentin, threw it to the sun, and put some in his mouth and on the crown of his head. If he became tired during a march or after combat, a bit of hoddentin on his tongue revitalized him. When the men returned safely to camp, they threw pollen to the sun and to the four directions—north, south, east, west—as a gesture of gratitude. If a fighter had been wounded, a medicine man who accompanied the war party prayed aloud for the warrior's recovery. As the healer walked back to the camp in front of the injured person resting on his horse, the holy man sprinkled pinches of hoddentin at intervals to ensure that their path homeward would be safe.

Praying was a large part of every Apache's daily life. One former Mexican captive explained the respect behind their frequent praying, saying, "We ask the favour of God. By his favour we exist always. The word of God is good. Although God has not put water on our heads (that is, baptized us), God will always be kind to us. When God wills a man shall die, he dies. If God wants a man to live to be old, he will live . . . God sees all. He hears all."[25]

Apaches have been reverent throughout their history; all Apache mothers teach their children to pray. Prayer and praying is the basis of an all-pervasive spirituality that women of the tribe kept alive by instructing the children. In many cultures, hunting, for example, is sport, and participants must obtain permission to take part from one of their authorities. Not so in the Apache way. To them, stalking game through the forest was a spiritual experience for both men and women. The women who stayed at home while the men roamed the region in search of food prayed every morning for four days after the men left, including while cooking and tending the fire.

Cooking, accompanied by prayers, was a natural extension of a woman's role, complementing the hunter's, in gathering food. After praying to Ussen for a successful food-gathering expedition, the older women served as mentors, traveling with girls, supervising them, answering their questions, teaching them the correct prayers, and instructing the girls in identifying various plants and how to shell, hull, husk, and strip wild foods to obtain the edible parts. Mescal, for example, was an Apache staple produced by century plants that all the women gathered. When it was ready for cooking, the woman prayed as she soaked the mescal in water, cut its stalks and crowns, roasted it in pits a young man dug for her, and then mixed it with berries and nuts, some of which had been packed away with wild onions the women had picked the year before.

Apache women made soup from white roots and tubers boiled with chunks of meat. The white flowers of the yucca cactus were also boiled, dried, and stored. Unopened yucca buds were split and dried as sweetening for hot herbal teas. Seeds, wild raspberries and strawberries, acorns, beans, chokecherries, and potatoes were picked or dug up, either to be prepared right away or stored for future consumption. Acorns were mixed with meat and fat, rolled into a ball, and given to the men to take on hunts or raids.

Wild grasses and crushed potatoes formed a flour that served as the basis for bread, which often contained ground berries and beans as well. Honey was spread on the bread, having been carefully removed directly from the comb after smudge fires had smoked the bees out. Young women or boys shot arrows that tore off chunks of the hive that were then squeezed until the honey dripped into bags. Women also collected wild tobacco while in search of food.[26] When the gathering had been successful and the foodstuffs brought into the encampment, no doubt more prayers were offered, some to the four directions.

Bourke noted the prevalence of a symbol—the cross—in the Apache culture, observing that it was related to the cardinal points and the four winds. Warriors painted the symbol on their moccasins before going into a strange area in the hope of keeping them from traveling on a wrong trail.

In October 1884 Bourke saw a procession of Apache men and women led by medicine men bearing two crosses. They were made of a vertical arm four feet ten inches long and a transverse between ten and twelve inches. Each was made of slats about one and a half inches wide, decorated with blue polka dots on the unpainted surface, and looked to him as if they had been long in use. A blue snake meandered down the longer arm. A circle of small willow twigs was pasted above a small, zinc-cased mirror, a bell, and eagle feathers. Bourke thought this particular cross might have represented a composite of the original Apache beliefs about the symbol, begun on the Spanish colonial frontier, coupled with and modified by the ideas of the Mexican captives among them who still remembered the Roman Catholic doctrine they had learned there.[27]

Mortuary practices were also a component of traditional Apache religion and not related at all to the Christian rites Spaniards performed and imposed. Chiricahua Apaches believe that at death they are transformed, and their spirits begin a four-day journey to the spirit world. Open burial sites are very dangerous between the moment of death and when the grave is covered or the corpse is lowered into mountain crevices, as on the frontier, for the spirit is loose and free, able to cause mischief or harm. Traditional funeral rites are intended to expedite the journey and keep the newly departed spirits from being lonely enough to come back to earth and conscript loved ones to go along with them. While not sacred in the same way as some other geographical sites, graves are places of transformation where journeys to the spirit world have been undertaken.

A female relative of the deceased ordinarily readied a body for burial but not with any willingness, for Apaches were reluctant to touch their dead. Still, a woman always stepped forward to do it, often the deceased's sister. One practice called for bathing the body, combing the hair, and placing red paint on the dead person's face. Then the female mortician dressed the deceased in attractive clothing. A male relative mounted him on his horse, sat behind him to hold him up, and rode the horse to the burial site where the body would be interred, probably on the same day as the death. If an aboveground burial was planned, members of the burial party wrapped the body in a blanket, canvas, or hide, put brush under and over it, and placed a few rocks on top of it.

Sometimes they laid the body on a layer of rocks, piled brush on top, dropped leaves and dirt above that, and carefully set more rocks over all, forming a mound that, with a little luck, would not attract wildlife.[28] Throughout this activity, all the participants uttered prayers.

Depending on the character and quality of the terrain and the types and preponderance of wildlife, it could have been reckless to bury a body aboveground. The frontier soil in many places was extremely rocky and knotted with tough, gnarled roots, making it difficult, if not impossible, to dig a grave. Consequently, nearby caves and crevices were favored as burial sites that were then sealed with boulders.[29]

Chiricahua Apaches on the colonial frontier observed a period of mourning lasting about a year, and some families still honor this today, although modifications have been made through the years. A few contemporary Apaches remain influenced by the ancient custom that prohibited mentioning the deceased's name. Elbys Naiche Hugar, a great-granddaughter of Cochise explained. "Your dead relative may be very busy doing something important where he is and when he hears you speak his name, he'll be interrupted. He might not like that."[30]

In historical times, another constraint against speaking the dead person's name was a fear of ghost sickness, an ailment characterized by heart flutter and sudden unconsciousness, thought to be caused by annoying dead relatives and friends.[31] Although healers specialized in curing ghost sickness through dedicated prayers and ceremonies, tribal members took routine precautions to avoid becoming ill with this affliction. Burning clothing worn while performing any preburial task was one way of avoiding ghost sickness, and brushing their bodies with green grass at the grave site was another.

The uses of protections from harm and evil practiced in the unfamiliar surroundings were important cultural components and were coupled with a strong reliance on family to defeat any daily perils in the strange desert territory. Perry wrote, "In the beliefs of most Athapaskan peoples the universe was capricious, filled with unpredictable entities who could either help or harm human beings."[32] Those whose actions were hurtful in many ways were thought of as witches.

Traditional Chiricahua Apache customs told of the danger witches could wreak and offered guidelines for determining whether an individual—Indian or non-Indian—was a witch. For example, witches

Are friendly with ghosts
Don't take precautions when handling the dead
Use amulets
Spread sickness
Are troublemakers
Have strange habits
Act peculiarly
Wear beads openly
Dress differently
Are chronic beggars or misers
Are sexually aberrant—they don't live with women
Point with their fingers instead of lips
Sleep alone outdoors
Refuse to eat foods cooked by others
Dance naked in the woods
Talk about others in a cruel manner[33]

Obviously no person would fit all the descriptions that would also have to be accompanied by evil deeds, but it is easy to note the vague and general attributes. Guilty individuals were also identified through exhibiting unmistakable characteristics such as pointing with fingers, demonstrating a preference for sleeping alone outdoors, refusing to eat foods others cooked, dancing naked in the woods, or talking about someone else in a cruel manner; gossiping was permitted, provided it did not become too ugly.

The apparent generality of the characterizations is a clue to the frightening threats that witches and witchcraft presented to the colonial Chiricahua Apaches. Had the definition been more specific than general, the numbers of identified witches would have been fewer, but in that case, in the Apache way of thinking, more might have escaped detection. Thus it was necessary for the "net" to catch more, just so no one slipped through. By way of further explanation, Apaches saw danger lurking everywhere in their new environment and were learning how to survive by their wits, imagination, reliance on family members, cultural memories, and the advice and prayers their medicine men and medicine women offered.

Chiricahua Apaches believed their healers were blessed with talent that was different from that of all others in the tribe; they were able to fill many cultural roles. They were historians, knowledgeable about the tribe's evolution from the earliest times to the present. They were philosophers, providing explanations for the processes and existence of Apache life. They were the repositories of the legends and myths from the distant past. They were physicians, supplying the means of curing illnesses. They were genealogists, familiar with each family's genetic makeup, an important attribute within a small group. They were counselors, offering relevant social consultation. They were wise leaders who had the community's respect in offering solutions to individual and collective problems. Especially, because of their intimate relationship with the Creator and the tribal belief that the Creator supported and sustained their connection, they were without equals.

"Medicine men and women hold great power," said an anonymous Mescalero Apache woman to researcher Teresa Pijoan, a native of San Juan Pueblo in New Mexico.

> The White Eyes [Euro-Americans] people never understood nor respected them. Medicine people brought healing, held Power, helped make decisions in the group. Medicine people taught children how to heal with herbs, how to use plants and teas for cures . . . Medicine people work with plants, herbs, songs, chants, heat, cold, and spirit . . . Medicine people know it is spirit that is hurt or being evil. They work on this. They heal this. Ussen gives power to heal.[34]

A major responsibility of medicine people was and still is participation in the ancient puberty ceremony, the best example of a traditional ritual that combines all three sacred elements of prayers, songs, and blessings. The rite antedates any contact with other indigenous groups or ethnic Europeans, having been given to the Chiricahua Apaches in the time before time by White Painted Woman in order to ensure to continuation of the tribe and prepare the young woman for a useful, abundant life.

In her instructions to the Chiricahua Apaches, White Painted Woman's exact words were, "We will have the girls' puberty rite. When the girls first menstruate, you shall have a feast. There shall be songs for the girls. During this feast, the *Gahe* [Mountain Spirit dancers] shall dance in front. After that there shall be round dancing and face to face dancing."[35]

Puberty ceremonies were and still are a joyful, essential, and spiritual part of becoming an adult female in the tribe, and the Apaches have continued the ceremony regardless of the external circumstances.[36] In keeping with the Chiricahua custom, another sacred tale about the puberty ceremony, different from the mandate by White Painted Woman, begins with the grandfather of the gods giving Old Woman a message for the Apaches. According to the tale, Old Woman found it difficult to keep up with other members of the tribe as they followed the animals and other sources of food. Exhausted, she fell by the wayside, and others moved on without her. She slept and fell into a coma. Suddenly a constant jingling penetrated her deathlike state and caused her to become instantly alert. She heard a spirit voice that described the process of the puberty ceremony and urged her to hurry and rejoin her tribe so she could instruct them. Revivified, Old Woman followed the directions.

No information is available that describes the maiden's clothing or the puberty ceremonies held in the cold country, but in northern Mexico the girl's puberty dress was made from doeskins or buckskins, starting with a large hide that was hand-tanned with an animal's brains and cut into two pieces, an upper blouse and a lower skirt. The tail of a black-tailed doe was suspended from the back hem of the blouse. Usually the girl's mother, grandmother, or another female relative fringed the hide, sewed a tiny jingle to each fringe, and decorated the dress. Some dresses kept their natural color, and some were painted with strips of green or yellow; the maiden's wishes determined the color. The dress was blessed by having someone sing for it, usually an older woman who began her songs as long as two months in advance of the scheduled ceremony and was paid in foods or medicines for her services.

About a year before the event, the girl's parents and relatives stored various foods such as piñon nuts, mesquite beans, yucca, and fruit. According to tradition, family members would eventually prepare and serve them all at the ceremony.

Whenever or wherever it is held, the ceremony begins at dawn of the first day when a girl's sponsor bathes her and instructs her in the words that are necessary to start the celebration of her womanhood. The sponsor then dresses the girl, who faces the east. The sponsor then prays and, starting from the right foot, places each item of clothing on the maiden's body. She drapes pieces of shells and necklaces of beads around the girl's neck, inserts earrings in her earlobes, and pins two black feathers from the tail of the female eagle into her hair.

To ensure that the girl will have a good appetite throughout her life, a medicine man or medicine woman feeds the young woman a piece of wild fruit, marked with a cross of pollen, as she prepares to leave her wickiup for the ceremonial grounds. The sponsor has already attached a reed and scratcher to her dress so that her lips will not touch water for four days nor her fingernails become dirty by scratching an itch. If the girl should make a mistake and drink water from a cup rather than through the reed, the belief is that she will invite rain, which in turn will impede the progress of the ceremony. Also, the sponsor tells the girl that she may not look at the sky or be disobedient for that will also cause rain clouds to gather. The sponsor warns the girl against laughing excessively, for such behavior will cause her to have a prematurely wrinkled face; any character traits a girl shows during the ceremony will distinguish her for the rest of her life. Hence, she may not lose her temper, make fun of anyone, or swear. She may talk a little, though, heed what she has been told, and maintain grave, dignified manners.

After the medicine men erect a tipi on the ceremonial grounds early on the first morning of the ritual, a girl and her sponsor come forward. The attendant places a tanned hide on the ground, and the maiden kneels on it. Her sponsor marks her face and body with pollen, after which the girl does the same to the older woman. When the painting is done, the maiden lies on the hide and is rubbed from foot to head, from the right side to the left, by the attendant who simultaneously prays for the girl to have a good disposition, good morals, good health, and a long life.

The younger woman then runs four times around a woven basket, placed on the ground about thirty paces from the medicine tipi, to symbolize a woman's stages of life—infancy, childhood, adulthood, and old age. The runs also mark White Painted Woman's journey from the east, where she initially emerged as a beautiful young woman, walked across the spectrum of time to the west, and disappeared when elderly, before reappearing again as a youth in the east. Inside the basket are sacred items, including pollen, a deer or elk hoof rattle, and a bundle of grass and feathers. All represent each of the four days the Creator used to make the world and its occupants.

After each single run, the basket is moved closer to the sacred tipi so that after the last run the girl picks up the basket and holds it to each of the four directions in clockwise order, starting with the south. This gesture ensures that any sickness or ailment that might harm her is chased away. The run itself demonstrates the maiden's physical fitness, so important to the girl and the future of the tribe.

After nightfall on each of the four nights, the maiden kneels in the rear of the medicine tipi in front of a low fire burning in a central fire pit. Medicine men sing *sotto voce* in accompaniment to the sounds made by shaking deer hoof rattles. At a designated point in the service the girl begins to dance and continues for hours with little relief except for an occasional rest period. This exhausting activity demonstrates her endurance, a quality much desired in all Apache women.

About ten minutes before sunrise on the fifth morning, one of the medicine men begins the closing ceremony by painting an outline of the sun on the palm of his left hand just as the sun approaches the medicine tipi's east entryway. At that exact moment, he rubs his hands over the head and face of the girl—who has spent the previous night in the tipi—before using a brush of gramma grass into which an eagle feather has been inserted to paint the girl's face, arms, and legs. On the right side of her face he also paints stripes of red and white, representing the rainbow. As the girl leaves the sacred tipi, Apache women carry baskets of food onto the ceremonial grounds and place them in a single line running eastward from the fire pit. The observers gather around, and the food is distributed. The medicine men mark the final closure of the ceremony by dismantling the sacred tipi.

Theoretically and practically, the puberty ceremony shows Apache girls the way toward a good life by its emphasis on four all-important life objectives: physical strength, a good disposition, prosperity, and a sound and healthy, uncrippled old age. The phases of the ritual associated with massage and running symbolically provide the young woman with the physical strength needed for her life ahead. A pleasant attitude promises that the girl will always have the support and assistance of her relatives. Prosperity is measured in freedom from hunger and an adequate supply of meat for her family despite ever-present environmental dangers, and living to an old age is viewed as evidence of victory over all the dark forces in the universe designed to do harm.

As an integral part of the entire puberty ceremony, the Mountain Spirit dancers assist the maiden to become a woman in the eyes of the tribe. The dancers impersonate the Mountain Spirits, a race of supernaturals who dwell within many mountains, according to Chiricahua Apache belief. There they are said to live and conduct their affairs much as the Apache used to do in aboriginal times. In dance, the men are masked and appear with their bodies painted in various patterns. "This procedure or rite is expected to establish rapport between a shaman and the original supernaturals from whom he gained his power and to enlist the aid of the Mountain Spirits" in celebration of the maiden's passage into womanhood.[37]

The origin of these legendary holy people reaches back to a time before time. One sacred story describes two young Apache men who were physically disabled, one blind and the other lame. Because of their handicaps, they could not keep up with the tribe during warfare, and so they had to be left behind after one particular battle. Warriors placed them together in a hillside cave with enough food and water to keep them well supplied until someone returned for them.

The two sat closely together in the dark cave, fearing they would be taken captive at any moment by their enemies. Many days and weeks passed, and they slowly lost hope of ever being reconciled with their families. One evening, shortly after dusk, the men heard strange noises and worried that their hiding place had been discovered. The unfamiliar sound came closer and closer until it suddenly stopped right at the entrance to the cave, where five figures of men who seemed unreal were strangely clad in exotic outfits composed of kilts made of deerskin, belts of hide, and high-legged, buckskin moccasins. They wore black masks over their faces. Their bodies were individually decorated with symbols representing corn, wind, and rain. No two looked alike. They wore great headdresses of wooden slats painted with symbolic figures. In each hand they held jagged staves; the right one had a cross painted on it, representing the four directions. Standing between the figures of the gods was a small form, masked but without headdress. He spoke to the men and urged them not to be afraid, for they all had come from the four directions to relieve them of their suffering and deliver them safely to their people.

The five began to dance around a fire that had suddenly come up, as had the winds and the rain, bringing food and life. At regular intervals the figures uttered a soft cooing sound, like the voice of a woman. The dancers chanted continuously and waved their staves to drive away the evil spirit that had made one man blind and the other lame. When the dance ended, the holy people led the two handicapped men through the entrance out onto a trail toward a huge rock that overlooked the cave they were living in. The dancer who was painted white hit the rock with his stave and it split, opening a passageway through which all entered. While walking this path, the blind man regained his vision, and the lame man was once again able to walk normally. To their astonishment, they were also beautifully clothed in buckskins and held the finest curved bows and arrows in their hands. When they turned to thank the dancers, no one was in sight. Looking to the east they saw an encampment of tipis and found their people.

Shortly after the men were reunited with their tribe, the dance of the Mountain Spirits was performed for the first time outside the cave. Each step of the dance, as described by the two men, was carefully followed. Groups of dancers eventually formed, headed by leaders the two men chose.[38]

Caves in mountainsides are places of power in the Chiricahua Apache spiritual belief system, possibly because White Painted Woman hid her child from danger in a cave. One powerful view of caves is that they were looked upon as portals to the underworld, a spirit dimension in rough contrast to the Christian concept of heaven. Opler recorded two myths about women who visited the underworld, both finding that "the same conditions as are found in this world prevail there" and "the people were living there just as we live here."[39] Another Chiricahua Apache concept of caves is that they sheltered and protected the people from harm and served as a storage place for weapons, clothing, and food, reflecting one reason, in the Chiricahua Apache view, why Ussen wanted the people to live in the Southwest, where caves in the mountains are abundant.

There is also a tale about a water monster who lived in a water hole near Deming, New Mexico. The Chiricahua Apaches on the Spanish colonial frontier were reluctant to go there because of its reputation as a dangerous place, but, according to the tale, one courageous young woman approached the spot to fill her water jug. The monster grabbed her, and she was never seen again. After a ceremony was conducted, the girl's father went to the water hole and saw his daughter emerge. She spoke to him, promising that if he stayed with her at the site no harm would come to him. He lived there for a while and then wandered away, only to be killed by Mexicans.[40] This story connects water with ongoing life and cautions listeners to exactly follow the advice given them at sacred sites.

Also alerting the people to the spiritual significance of water was an old mythological tale involving a coyote. Opler reported that a raven threw a stick in the water and said, "If it sinks, there is going to be death, but if not, everything will be all right." The stick floated. Then Coyote came along and said the same thing about a rock, threw it in the water, and it sank. "After that the people began to die off."[41] The story conveyed the principle of respect for the waterways in order to avoid death.

While certain waterways in the desert took on spiritual meaning because of the events that occurred there, the pragmatic Apaches revered water for without sources ranging from dripping springs to flowing rivers in the desert, they could not survive. Waterways were always considered sources of spiritual power, Carmichael wrote, because they provided "contact with the spiritual dimension inasmuch as the water has just emerged from within the earth. Power from the spirit world is carried into the physical world by the flowing water."[42]

Birthplaces are an example of holy sites that remain in family memories through oral history, oral tradition, or oral testimony. "Apaches regarded their birthplace with special attachment," reported Angie Debo. "The child was always told of the location, and whenever in its roving the family happened by, he was rolled on the ground there to the four directions. This observance took place throughout the growing years, and even adults sometimes rolled in this manner when returning to the spot where they were born."[43]

Traditional Chiricahua Apaches, whether ancestral or contemporary, have always had a very personal relationship with the spirit world. While the concept of spiritual geography—holy sites at the intersection of the spiritual and material worlds—was not unique to the diverse Indian populations in the Spanish colonial frontier, many saw the entire environment as a source of physical and spiritual sustenance. The Chiricahua Apaches knew their territory, the landforms, the waterways, the flora and the fauna, and the earth, in an intimate way. These were thought of in a *qualitative* sense, as having been given to them by Ussen with the expectation that they would interact with their surroundings in a positive, harmonious way. When this happened, when individuals or groups sought solace or respite at a particular location, they were frequently rewarded with spiritual experiences that marked the site forever in personal, familial, and tribal memory.

When the religious Spaniards first arrived in northern Mexico in the early to mid-1600s, they had no idea about the power of the Chiricahua Apaches' spiritual background, nor did they care. Even though they were armed with the egocentricity conferred by empire and the "dominion" as promised in Genesis, the Europeans would discover that these particular indigenous people, whom they were sworn to convert to Christianity, had absolutely no regard for them or for their religion. The Apaches were content with what Ussen had designated for them and were determined to protect it at any cost, setting the stage for inevitable conflict.

Missions and Missionaries

⅋ JUST ABOUT THE TIME THE APACHE SOUTHWARD MIGRATION REACHED northern Mexico, religious activities in Rome laid the foundation for missionary efforts in the same area. Pope Julius II's 1508 papal bull created the concept of royal patronage (*patronato real*), which, according to Kieran McCarty, OFM, was

> a legally regulated grant from the church to the crown. The crown became the pope's representative in the Spanish New World primarily because of its willingness to support the missionary endeavor with funds from the royal treasury. Thus it was that the missionaries, whose principal task was to bring word of the good news of Christ to the uninitiated, also became agents of the Spanish king. They were appointed to bring about the cultural assimilation of the native population.[1]

Under this authority, Spain, a Roman Catholic nation, gained the legitimacy to eradicate the traditional ancestral lifeways of indigenous peoples and force an alien religion on them, through slavery if necessary. Worse, agents of the Roman Catholic Church, the Jesuit and Franciscan missionaries, would eventually sell human beings to meet the challenges.

Pope Paul III, on September 27, 1540, approved the formation of the Company of Jesus that became known as the Jesuits. Founded by St. Ignatius of Loyola, the organization's specific purpose was to propagate and strengthen the Roman Catholic faith everywhere, so from the very beginning the worldwide missionary labors of the Jesuits consisted of preaching, teaching catechism, administering the sacraments, and conducting missions. Thus, the Jesuits were, at least theoretically, well suited for northern Mexico, where most of the thousands of inhabitants from many Indian tribes had no idea of Christianity.

The Jesuits' assignment to northern Mexico was the result of a shortage of diocesan, secular priests. Regular clergy, those belonging to religious orders, were free from the control of bishops, an important concept on the remote Spanish colonial frontier. Secular clergy were under the direct authority of the bishops whom the king and his deputies appointed. Had there not been a slump in the number of available clergy, the papacy would have continued its reliance on diocesan priests to carry the Word into northern Mexico. Because of the circumstances, however, a papal bull in 1546 granted the Jesuits permission to indoctrinate the indigenous peoples of an area they called the Pimería Alta into Christianity, administer the sacraments, educate the Indians, and prepare them for citizenship. Evangelizing started in earnest in the mid-1600s at a site named Ures.

In 1628, 382 Jesuits working in the Pimería Alta received an annual stipend of 250 pesos each from the royal treasury, which also furnished bells, chalices, vestments, and other items necessary for a mission to function. By 1645 there were thirty-five Jesuit missions in the Mexican states of Sinaloa and Sonora, each consisting of from one to four sites where an adobe church and quarters for the priest were located.

Proof of their religious, political, and cultural superiority was obvious to the occupiers: they were better educated, had better weapons than the Indians, were skilled in working metal to produce tools, had domesticated horses for transportation and raised other livestock for food, and were knowledgeable in the mass production of other subsistence crops through "modern" farming techniques. In addition, their language was written, and some citizens could read and write, an unmistakable sign of supremacy in their eyes over the indigenous peoples.

Nicholas Bleser noted an underlying premise that added to the Spaniards' egocentrism. "The basic Spanish assumption was that the Indians either had no political organization or that which they did have was a primitive and inferior version of the Spanish or other European systems."[2] Had these foreigners been at all interested, they would have recognized that the native sociopolitical and religious structures in place had satisfied the needs of these indigenes for centuries. Would it have made any difference to them? Possibly, although not everyone would agree with me. Nonetheless, the newcomers to northern Mexico would have realized that the indigenes had a system of governance that was suitable politically because it worked well and that could have ameliorated their vanity somewhat.

Totally disregarding the Indians' established lifeways, the Spaniards expected them to meet four obligations: to recognize the king as owner of all the land and as the supreme authority on earth; accept a simplified local system of Spanish government; accept Christianity in the form of Roman Catholicism; and recognize the missionaries as their spiritual and moral leaders.[3]

Even though the four premises were specifically designed to introduce the Indians of northern Mexico to Christianity, each was not without impediments. Ward Churchill identified one of the first problems during that time as a question of whether the natives of the New World were endowed with souls and could therefore become Christians. The outcome of a famous debate in Valladolid, Spain, about this heated topic was "the recognition that the Indians were human beings and entitled to exercise at least rudimentary rights." So, among other conclusions reached, including yes, they had souls, the debate also recognized that natives had property rights. Spanish legal theorists added, however, that the Indians' "discoverers" had other powers to "acquire the property from its native owners, in the event they could be persuaded through peaceful means to alienate it."[4] In complete disregard of the new legal concept of aboriginal title and its derivations, Christian missionaries removed the natives from their villages through a policy of *reducción/ congregación*, "reducing" the native villages and "congregating" the indigenes in missions where they were made to work under strict supervision. Bluntly speaking, the Indians were forced out of their villages and into confinement where an unfamiliar authority demanding obedience oversaw them. Not to be overlooked in importance, reducción vacated Indian lands for incoming Spaniards to appropriate.

The late Charles W. Polzer, SJ, a noted Jesuit authority, explained that "the intention behind forming reducciones was to lead the Indian

. . . into a community where he could better learn the rudiments of Christian belief and the elementary forms of Spanish social and political organization."[5] He did not mention land appropriation, nor did he discuss the regimentation and discipline the missionaries imposed as necessary for the long-term success if these religious representatives of the empire were to realize two major goals: converting the Indians into Christians and shaping them into tax-paying citizens.

Should any Indians resist the change and voice a desire to return, military personnel were garrisoned in nearby presidios to enforce the missionaries' wishes and, not incidentally, to protect everyone from other Indians' assaults.[6] The presence of soldiers, their uniforms, their horses, their sounds, their drills, their weapons, their strange appearance, and their foreign language should have been enough to intimidate and quiet any dissent, but in some cases it was not. Despite the intimidation, many Indians still subscribed to their shamans' instructions to resist the Europeans. In that case, wrote Robert Perez, "the missionaries lamented that it was impossible to reduce [indigenes] to Spanish law without the aid of the military . . . In particular, the soldiers were to seek out any Native shamans that they could identify and make examples of them through public beatings."[7] Since the Christian agents of the cross and crown did not do the actual beatings, according to Polzer, it is possible that in their minds they excused themselves from any guilt.[8]

Although the New Laws of the Indies, promulgated in 1542, had declared that the Indians should not be mistreated, made to move, or work against their will, many of the frontier missionaries ignored the legality and concluded otherwise. For practical reasons, it was necessary that these future Christians be assembled where indoctrination, supervision, physical labor, and social control could be exercised.

Mission sites were deliberately chosen by the priests to confront the natives' age-old spiritual traditions head on. Many of the locations had been Indian ceremonial areas and sacred places. Gambling correctly that this unmistakable demonstration of their authority would overwhelm the Indians, the priests first erected ramadas, temporary shelters made of poles and brush, that would ultimately be replaced by adobe buildings, constructed through Indians' forced labor. As they stood under the ramadas, the priests read aloud in Spanish to a preliterate people the legal documents authorizing these activities, one of the strangest happenings

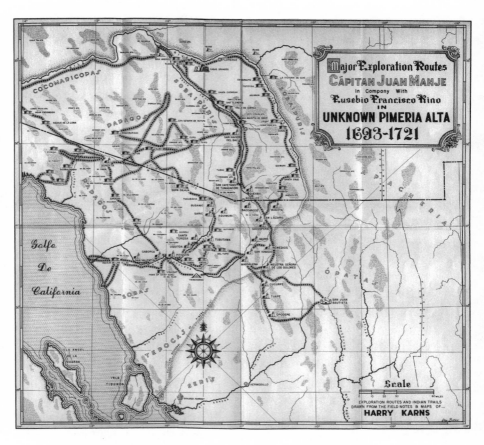

MAP 1 ❧ "Major Exploration Routes: Capitán Juan Manje In Company With Eusebio Francisco Kino in Unknown Pimería Alta, 1693–1721." From Harry J. Karns, *Luz de Tierra Incognita: Juan Mateo Manje; Unknown Arizona and Sonora, 1693–1701* (Tucson: Arizona Silhouettes, 1954).

on the colonial frontier. For all the effect this had, the Indians might as well have been deaf. Surely the Jesuits were intelligent human beings who knew that their words had absolutely no meaning to the indigenes, yet their fidelity to the cross and crown and its requirements superseded their own intellectual and common sense.

When the mission area was ready, congregación kept the subjugated Indians densely packed in working communities where religious indoctrination, careful supervision, and unlimited control over the indigenes' activities could be exercised by the missionaries. Before actual congregación, however, basic living areas within the mission complex had to be created, preferably near flowing water for sanitation and irrigation. First clearing the land required very hard work from the Indians, digging up roots and rocks with makeshift or unfamiliar European tools.

When the priests clashed with the mission residents, especially those who resisted the demand for hard work, established rules and precepts dictated the type of discipline to be meted out to unruly or uncooperative Indians. The father provincial, Andrés Xavier García, on June 25, 1747, set the Jesuits' standards: "If an Indian is to be punished for an ordinary fault, he will not receive more than 6 lashes. A more serious fault, 12; and the most serious, 25. In case they are women, never more than 8 and always at the hands of the governor or fiscal."[9] It must have been particularly confusing for the offending natives to understand discipline when they could not understand the error. Many, but not all, Indians eventually acquiesced to the Jesuits' orders rather than defy them in their strange new setting.

The next challenges included preparing for essential needs such as food and shelter. An important aspect of the Spanish plan for the use of the frontier was to introduce European crops, farming techniques, tools, and domesticated animals into the mission setting. Once reducción and congregación were accomplished, food production using forced Indian labor would begin. In the Spaniards' view, farming would produce an adequate food supply for the mission and perhaps even surplus crops in the future.

One group of natives dug, scraped, and moved the claylike, rocky soil to level the land and baked adobe bricks for a church building and the ancillary structures.[10] Others plowed and planted the fields in squash, garlic, melons, onions, corn, beans, and wheat when the harsh soil permitted. A third unit sawed and dragged tree limbs to be used as building material for huts that served as the indigenes' homes and for the roofs of several other structures, including the church and priests' houses, that comprised the mission complex.

The natives were not novice farmers. Long before contact with the Europeans they had broken the ground, planted maize, beans, squash, and other staples of their existence, but using European tools was a new experience. Whether the allure of learning how to handle the new equipment offset the priests' demand for long days of labor may never be known. Theodore Treutlein wrote that "the missionaries speak of communal agriculture as absolutely vital to the survival of the mission, a contention which was recognized by the crown, for a royal decree permitted each missionary to use the services of his Indians three days a week for the general improvement of the mission."[11] In his spare time, each mission Indian also tilled his own plot of land, if he had any energy left, cultivating his favorite foods and fruits like watermelon, cantaloupe, and other melons.

Wheat was one of the principal crops the native workers grew on mission lands, planted after oxen and wooden plows opened the soil.[12] Workers scattered seeds, then covered them over; hand-dug irrigation canals funneled river water to the field. Robert West wrote that to harvest the grain, "the Indians were taught to use the iron sickle and threshing was accomplished on the *era*, a hard surfaced spot, by driving the mules over the sheaves. Finally the grain was separated from the straw and the chaff by winnowing."[13]

Initially, large, roaming, domesticated animals such as cattle, horses, and mules brought to northern Mexico stepped freely across the landscape until the priests taught Indian men how to manage the livestock within a prescribed area, requiring indigenes to build corrals as adjuncts to the buildings they had already constructed. In time smaller animals such as sheep, goats, and chickens were added to the mix, and the responsibilities of the range workers increased.

Indigenes erected outlying buildings such as the priest's home, the novices' houses, the granary, the storerooms, the music room, the kitchen, liaison Indian officials' quarters, the blacksmith shop, and weaving and milling rooms. Since there was no set number of structures to be built in any of the missions, the overall size of the each center depended on the estimated number of Indians to be converted, the health of the priests, their ambitions, and their abilities.

In time, protecting the missions from unfriendly Indian groups became necessary, so presidios with complements of from twenty to fifty soldiers were erected nearby. Referred to as *castillos* or *fortela-zas*, the outposts were viewed as "protective garrisons on frontiers,"[14] but were little more than the captain's residence, the guardhouse, and the chapel.[15] These presidios were also "a basic social institution of colonization in the New World," according to Max Moorhead.[16] Physically representing the power and authority of the beloved Spain, the presidio became the hub of activities, a gathering spot for homesick settlers and a coming-together site for the re-creation of familiar public European rituals, particularly since the Pimería Alta was so geographically widespread.[17]

Many times the presidios did not effectively deter Indian raids, however, and the soldiers were often outnumbered; desertions were a fact. Poorly trained and paid a pittance, sometimes the "soldiers were so frightened that they did not want to dismount," wrote Roberto Salmón.[18] It was obvious that a plan needed to be developed and implemented to convince the troops to risk their lives. Initially the enticement was free land that had been taken from the Indians, and, in time, it was not beyond belief for an indigene to be loaned out from forced labor at the mission to work for a newly arrived Spanish soldier on what had previously been one of the worker's, tribe's, or his family's sacred sites.

Presidial officers and enlisted men were permitted to retain title to their property for as long as they remained at the presidio and that, depending on the individual, was often not a very long time. Salmón described the citizen soldiers as "settler-stockmen types . . . mediocre . . . but with a natural ability born of a rugged existence . . . local veci-nos comprised most presidial companies . . . The frustration of presidial service held for the soldier boredom, impoverished living conditions, constant drudge labor and deadening fatigue."[19]

When the soldiers voluntarily left their post or were transferred elsewhere, the title to their land but not their Indian workers was automatically applied to their replacements. If there were crops on the land, the new owners were expected to compensate the former owners. When an officer retired from military service, he was required to surrender his land even though he remained to live in the settlement. If an entire company was disbanded because the presidio was moved or closed, the soldiers were obligated to stay behind as settlers while the officers could stay on or move elsewhere. These men and their families, mainly Roman Catholic, needed the religious services of the missionaries, thus increasing the duties of the priests.

The Jesuits

Under the papal bull of 1546, granting the Jesuits permission to indoctrinate native peoples into Christianity, the missionaries instructed the Indians in the Spanish language, how to live indoors, and how to dress comfortably in European clothing and demonstrated the many ways of expressing loyalty to the king, for example, by obeying the clergy. Of supreme importance, however, was converting the indigenes to Roman

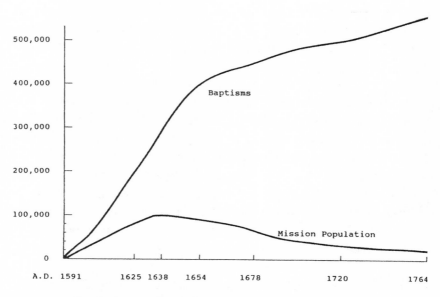

FIGURE 1 ∞ "Jesuit Baptisms and the Mission Population, 1591–1764."
From Daniel T. Reff, *Disease, Depopulation, and Culture Change in Northwestern New Spain, 1518–1764* (Salt Lake City: University of Utah Press, 1991).

Catholicism, whether or not they understood its tenets and obligations. The priests were to keep statistics listing the number of baptisms, voluntary or involuntary, and their "successes."[20] Failures could be deduced from the numbers.

Understanding and accepting their sacred duty, to a man the Jesuit trailblazers were ready to create and sustain a "Christian [Catholic] evolution" in the Pimería Alta, Spain's farthest colonizing Christian venture on the northwestern frontier.[21] The newly arrived priests initially became active in Ures, Sonora, in 1636, but it was not until 1687 when the venerable Eusebio Kino, SJ, appeared on the frontier that the pace of activities quickened. After Kino's death in 1711 progress continued in high gear. "By 1730," wrote Perez, "the province of Sonora contained sixty-six official Indian pueblos [missions?] under the administration of twenty-four missionaries."[22]

There was no question that the Jesuits were equal to their daunting job. As Donald Cutter and Iris Engstrand noted, the priests were men of "individual courage, crusading spirit, and disdain for the comforts of life," but after the initial excitement of the challenge abated some of these religious pioneers became disillusioned by the wide range of what was expected of them.[23] For example, the Swiss Jesuit, Felipe Segesser, wrote

> there remains little time to the father missionary for the performance of his spiritual labors . . . In order to write these fugitive lines . . . I had to set aside other business . . . Let us imagine that . . . I have earned an opportunity to say my [breviary] prayers. Along comes the cook and demands pepper, ginger, and saffron. The house servant announces that two messengers have arrived . . . While I say my prayers the houseboys set the table for luncheon. Now knives, and at other times forks, are not placed . . . [24]

Yet the circumstances were occasionally even more difficult than a frustrated Segesser reported. Hear the words of a Jesuit superior in Mexico City, writing anonymously in 1757, describing his version of what missionary life in northern Mexico entailed.

FIGURE 2 ∞ "Padre Kino as depicted by the El Paso artist, José Cisneros."
From George B. Eckhart, "A Guide to the History of the
Missions of Sonora, 1614–1826," *Arizona and the West* 2 (1960).

Their lives are filled with bitter disappointment and continual mortification. Aside from the headaches of mission administration and caring for souls; the ponderous studying of a barbarian tongue without the aid of teacher or books; the personal hardships which the mission's location and climate offer in the way of ruggedness and precipitousness, fording of swollen rivers without bridges or boats, oppressive and extreme heat, vermin and poisonous creatures, the rudeness and offensiveness of native character, the want of essentials and necessities; aside from all these there are other circumstances which provide an abundant harvest of suffering . . .[25]

These comments of Ignacio Xavier Keller, SJ, the depressed priest at the mission called Santa María Suamca, show his disappointment at his assignment.

All I received were uncivilized and scattered Indians. I had the winds to breathe with nothing more for sustenance. I had the open country in which to sleep, with no cover but the heavens . . . My neophytes had no oxen, nor did they know how to plow, until two years later when I acquired four . . . Because of the lack of provisions I was not able to go ahead with the building of a church, not even a house. Thus I persevered living for years in a straw-thatched hut like the natives, sustaining myself and them on the alms I would go out to beg for . . .[26]

This sounds dismal, but the indigenes were also having their share of gloom. Around the mid-1700s the glow of Christianity had faded for some mission Indians. The priests' bribery in the form of gifts to entice the indigenes into the missions and ensure their cooperation was no longer as effective as it initially had been, and more and more natives were avoiding baptism and refusing to be married in the church. A few unhappy Pimas living near San Xavier del Bac had aligned themselves with the Apaches, one of only a few resistant native groups. By March 1747, Perez reported, "sentiment against the missionaries was so high that [they] could go no where without a military escort," despite the fact that a frontier priest had to have almost superhuman fearlessness in the presence of Indians determined to drive him away.[27]

Courage is a significant attribute to appreciate, as it included the unflinching bravery the Jesuits needed to endure the rigors and perils of evangelizing amid unpredictable peoples in an unfamiliar, dangerous territory. Andrés Perez de Ribas, Mexico City's Jesuit provincial in the mid-1600s, described another component of the priests' courage.[28] He believed that "the Jesuit experience in the New World reflected the unfolding of a divine plan" and that the Jesuits accepted the possibility of martyrdom because they believed "they were living out their lives in fulfillment of a prophecy, continuing the work of Christ and his disciples."[29] This extreme view explains a religious individual's willingness to expose himself to continuing danger, but it still leaves one wondering about that person's psychological need to choose that way of life in the first place.

Another aspect of the missionaries' fortitude was permission to act as required with no constraints on the frontier, that is to say, any means to an end. Legally, through a nine-hundred-word manifesto, drawn up in 1514 and called the Requerimiento, all agents of the empire, including the Jesuits, were granted the legitimacy to do whatever was necessary to indoctrinate the Indians. In part, the document mandated the Indians to acknowledge the Roman Catholic Church and the pope as the ruler of the world and allow the faith to be preached to them. So that there would be no misunderstanding among the Indians about the Europeans' superiority, the Requerimiento asserted that the highest pinnacle of humankind was Jesus Christ, who ultimately transferred his power to St. Peter, who then bequeathed authority to the popes; Pope Alexander VI subsequently bestowed the American continent upon the Spaniards.

In a bizarre effort to establish the Requerimiento's authority and the priests' preeminence over indigenous peoples, this elaborate dictum was recited many times in the presence of Indians. The puzzled people heard unintelligible words to the effect that they must "accept the domination of the Spanish crown and embrace Christianity. If they resisted, their lands would be taken from them and they would be killed or enslaved . . . Christianity thus imbued Spaniards with a powerful sense of the righteousness of their aggression against those natives in North America who threatened to block their advance."[30]

For a justification that superseded all earthly means of conferring authority all that was needed was the Bible. In Genesis 1:26–28, on the fifth day of creation, God gives [man] dominion "over all the earth." Surely, from the Spaniards' point of view, biblical permission and royal documents sanctified any and all actions toward the indigenes during missionization, regardless of laws that prohibited mistreatment of the indigenes.

The word "mission" produces many varying images and raises questions. What exactly was a mission? It is important to appreciate the varying descriptions of facilities and practices. Jesuit Polzer, naturally, viewed missions from a religious standpoint:

> A mission may be a group of persons sent by the church to convert non-believers, or it may be the physical location in which conversion will take place, or it may be the buildings of a compound in which missionaries reside, or it may be all three. However, the object of a mission was to convert non-believers into believers, regardless of any forced cultural change that would take place.[31]

Oakah L. Jones Jr. concentrated on the numbers associated with missions, writing the Jesuits "established twenty-eight missions serving seventy-two [Indian] villages with a total population of 40,000 by 1678."[32]

Kidwell and her colleagues wrote that "the ultimate effect of Christian mission activity was to remove the Indian person from relationship to the tribal group in order to associate him or her with the artificial community of Christ."[33]

Robert Jackson took a political approach, noting that "although staffed by members of the Catholic Church, the mission was fundamentally a government institution funded by the Crown. The government had to authorize the establishment of each new mission."[34]

Lyle Williams approached the topic from a societal view, writing that "[missions] were unique to the Spanish Empire, having no antecedents or counterparts in any other area of the world" and that the "[mission] was not only a religious unit, but it was also a school—academic and vocational—an agricultural complex, a manufacturing center, and a settlement."[35]

Providing an alternate perspective, David Sweet declared

that the missions were more like the slave plantation or the high-land hacienda than like the semi-independent *pueblo de indios* of the colonial core areas, and more like the prison/reform school or the military base than like any other modern social institution . . . Indians for the most part settled in missions only after having been badly battered by disease, famine, enslavement, the intensification of intertribal war brought about by contact with the Europeans, war with the conquerors themselves, or some combination of these pressures.[36]

Although Sweet's conclusions express many of the negative circumstances of mission life, the Jesuits would have argued that the positive aspects of living among Europeans balanced Sweet's description: regular meals, clothing, education, music lessons, religious instructions, and some safety (albeit not guaranteed) from attack by enemies.

Protecting themselves from marauding tribes required constant vigilance, and in time the weary Jesuits tried a new approach: intervention to impose a period of peacefulness. Silvio Zavala wrote, "The authorities sometimes made brief alliances with the [attacking] Indians, giving them the necessities of life as presents in exchange for peace."[37] Bribery in the form of payoffs would be successful for a period of time, beyond which some tribal members would dismiss the priests' efforts to corrupt them.

Causing peace to break out through any means—remember, the Requerimiento endorsed whatever was necessary with no consequences to the priests for whatever methods they chose—would have been an enormous accomplishment, and saved many, many lives on the frontier. Jackson estimated that in the 1690s, approximately eighty-six hundred Indians, Pimas and others, lived or roamed where the Jesuits had initially organized their missions.[38] Would peace have meant more Indians coming to Christianity? Kay Parker Schweinfurth identified four elements influencing potential converts: the communication skills of the missionaries; the concrete symbols of a church's generosity—icons, gifts, and other material benefits (what I would call bribes); the extent to which concepts and rituals of Christianity were analogous to those of native religions; and the degree of tolerance the missionaries had for the integration and continuance of indigenous beliefs.[39]

The core of these components rested not with the Indians but on the priests' personalities—gregarious, outspoken, timid, antisocial, and all the other facets of an individual's singularity. Mood swings caused by the assignment's difficulty or by the area's remoteness affected the priests' daily mission life, as did achievements, poor health, frustrations, joy, zeal, and so forth. Illness was always an important issue. Some priests were so sick that they had to be transferred elsewhere, causing physical and psychological disruptions among the neophytes and in the missions' routines. One habit remained fairly constant, though: the priests' need to behave unethically in recruiting Indians to the mission life and Christianity. "Gift-giving . . . undoubtedly encouraged partial collaboration by the recipients," according to Susan Deeds.[40] This is an echo of Father Segesser's comments from the long ago: "Indians do not come to Christian service when they do not see the maize pot boiling."[41] One wonders if the priests' constant illnesses were related in any way to actions that were morally unacceptable, regardless of the legalities.

Bribery's limits were periodically reached as a result of geography, since the church's benevolence always depended upon supplies reaching northern Mexico in a timely fashion. Caravans from Mexico City, overloaded with provisions, were highly vulnerable to attack from hostile tribes so the largesse from which bribes were frequently allotted occasionally never arrived at all. Then the mission Indians were left empty-handed, some angry or frustrated that they had to wait up to one year for the next wagons. Many became disillusioned and discouraged with the church's unfulfilled promises, but they were trapped in the mission, unable to leave the compound without risking the undesirable consequences of being caught, returned, and punished. Some Indians loyal to the Spaniards understood and accepted the delay in receiving gifts, noting that their traditional religions occasionally resembled Christianity, and so saw no need to complain.[42]

Many curious indigenes living in the mission setting willingly participated in the required church services, testing the experience. Still others took the religious teachings seriously, regularly attended, allowed their children to join catechism classes, and learned Christian beliefs themselves. The religious exposure for these Indians became integrated into their hearts and minds, but the resisters demonstrated opposite reactions and drew punitive responses. Aware that the 1542 New Laws of the Indies prohibited disciplinary actions, the priests nonetheless applied reprisals in order to "break down the generational lines of authority in native society and to position themselves as the new leaders," wrote Charlotte Gradie.[43]

According to Nicholas Griffiths, "it is highly doubtful whether coercive methods had anything other than a negative impact on the Christianization of native peoples."[44] That is not absolutely true, though, for the degree of acceptance or rejection of the Europeans' religion was an individual decision. For some clever Indians, resisting the European appeared as overt acquiescence, actually "merely an outward appearance . . . a parallel universe . . . the outward commitment that allows for a layer of protection for traditional cultural values and the ceremonial forms that accompany those values."[45] At the other extreme, some indigenes honestly and wholeheartedly surrendered to the powerful images and symbols of Spanish authority. Accepting the indigenes' personal unpredictability was a key to understanding the people, as the Jesuits learned.

The language barrier added to the mutual difficulties. Different tribal dialects and tongues ranged all across northern Mexico. After a few false starts in communicating, the Spaniards solved the problem by speaking to the Indians in one language only—Spanish; lessons in the mission were mandatory. Indian children quickly caught on, and the adults followed albeit at a slower pace.

Another obstacle was geographical: the religious headquarters in Mexico City was three months' to one year's travel time away. While this distance provided the Jesuits with freedom from constant supervision, the remoteness affected the faraway officials' decisions about the frontier missionaries' needs. A mission's census often vacillated, showing a large population one month and then a dramatic reduction the next. To accommodate the former, a priest would send a long list of needed supplies to Mexico City, yet the accompanying census documents were incompatible, showing fewer residents at that moment and causing suspicions. By the time the often-disputed supplies arrived up to a year later, if at all, circumstances had changed more than once so the next order would be different again.

Continuing vulnerability to Indian assaults, even when not actively engaged in conflict, caused psychological stress, another obstacle that was debilitating for the priests and the mission Indians. For example, on November 30, 1749, Nicolás de Perera, SJ, stationed at Baviacora,[46] wrote to Father Segesser at Ures,[47] describing plans for a fiesta that he wanted to hold for the military personnel, the civilians, and the friendly Indians.[48] A little more than two weeks later, on December 17, 1749, in a letter to another priest, Father Segesser wrote that he had learned of the arrival at Ures of a squadron of soldiers to protect the civilian settlers and the missions against one of the more aggressive tribes, the Seris.[49] No doubt the fiesta was canceled.

Certainly the Indian raids were a serious and dangerous part of Jesuit mission life, and the frontier Apaches were only one tribe that attacked the Europeans. The Seris had been in open hostility against the Spanish since 1699; the Yaqui rebellion occurred in 1740; and the northern Pimas revolted in 1695, 1737, 1739, and 1751. Throughout the ongoing chaos, however, a carefully planned Jesuit mission building program, using forced Indian labor, proceeded intermittently as best it could despite bloody interruptions.

A look at several missions reveals the Jesuits' strong drive to fulfill their obligations. Much of the information below has been taken from four sources.[50]

Los Santos Ángeles de Guévavi

Eusebio Kino, SJ, first visited this site in 1690–91 when it was a Pima village. Ten years later Guévavi was a *cabecera*—headquarters for a number of outlying satellite missions called *visitas*—filled with Pimas reduced from their native settlements named Upiatuban and El Concuc and living at the nearby visitas of San Cayetano de Tumacácori, San Luis del Bacoancos, and Los Santos Reyes de Sonoita.[51] Pima workers built a small church and a house and then laid the foundations of a larger church. Jake Ivey reported that

> only the most basic tools were needed to construct a mission. A measuring cord, a simple A-frame leveling device, a plumb bob, hammers, picks, shovels, buckets, trowels, axes, saws, augurs, pulleys for lifting systems, stakes, and string were sufficient The [priest] had been trained to make baked brick, tile, and lime. Stone-cutting chisels, sledgehammers, and pry-bars were supplied if the buildings were to be of stone, or the [priest] taught

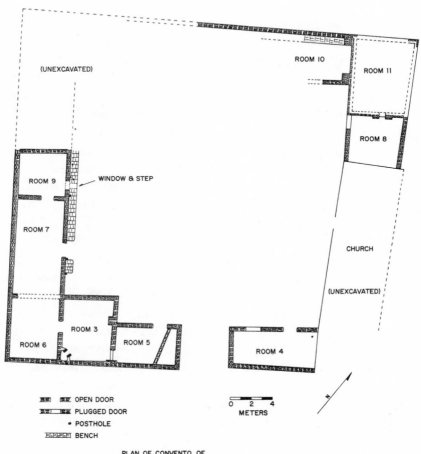

his building crew the methods of building wooden forms and making adobe bricks.[52]

The first resident priest, possibly Juan de San Martín, SJ, left before the end of 1701, probably because of illness and was not immediately replaced. The mission was administered from afar by Augustín Campos, SJ, and Ignacio Keller, SJ, resident missionaries at San Ignacio and Suamca. Johann Grazhoffer, SJ, was assigned to Guévavi in 1732 and baptized 978 people before he left.[53] It was he who added the name San Rafael to the mission, but in 1744 a different resident priest changed the name to San Miguel. Sometime in the 1740s the mission began to look official, and in the summer of 1751, Joseph Garrucho, SJ, oversaw elaborate plans to construct a major church, about fifteen by fifty feet. Don Joaquín de Casares of Arizpe, a master builder, arrived with his assistants, was joined by Pima workers, and construction began. The Pima revolt later that year caused some damage to the unfinished structure, but the building was not burned to the ground and remained upright. It was later patched and then renovated in 1754 under the watchful eye of Francisco Pauer, SJ. In 1767 its visitas were San Ignacio de Sonoitac, San José de Tumacácori, and San Cayetano del Calabazas. After the Franciscans arrived, Tumacácori became the cabecera in 1770–71. Guévavi was abandoned by 1776 for three reasons: an unhealthy climate, contagious diseases, and shamans and bewitchment.[54] The constant Apache assaults were no doubt also a determining cause for completely vacating the mission. Still visible today are portions of the church's adobe walls. Large, flat stones, scattered now all around, once served as the foundation for living quarters.[55]

San Cayetano de Calabazas

Francisco Pauer, SJ, conducted the first baptism here on April 20, 1756. Seven months later, on November 1, he moved seventy-eight Indians to this location atop a mesa on the east side of the Santa Cruz River, just upstream from Sonoita Creek. No religious structures were apparent until May 1761, when a half-built church sat near a new house with a door and lock. Although Calabazas's location on the bluff offered some protection from Indian assaults, it was under siege from Apaches for a number of years.

FIGURE 4 ∾ "Ruins of Calabazas mission." Photo by author.

San Xavier del Bac

On his first visit in 1692 to the site, now a few miles south of Tucson, the venerable Eusebio Kino, SJ, told the Pimas about

> how in ancient times the Spaniards were not Christians, how Santiago came to teach them the faith, and how for the first 14 years he was able to baptize only a few . . . but that the most holy Virgin appeared to him and consoled him, telling him that Spaniards would convert the rest of the people of the world . . . They listened with pleasure to these and other talks concerning God, heaven, and hell, and told me that they wished to be Christians, and gave me some infants to baptize.[56]

This description is remarkable, given the fact that the Pimas' Spanish language skills were limited, if present at all. It is probable that translators accompanied Kino on his visits to the villages, but there is no indication of that this time at Bac.

In 1700 indigenes laid the church's first adobe brick but work stopped for half a century because of Indian raids. In 1756 Alonso Espinosa, SJ, arrived and restarted construction. Indoor services were conducted by 1763, although architectural problems plagued the building from the beginning. Father Espinosa did not level the ground before construction began, and no stone foundations had been laid as footings to support the building. The completed church had two side chapels and a sacristy behind the sanctuary and main altar. Oddly, posts ran down the middle of the nave to the sanctuary.[57] There is no evidence today of any ruins of the Jesuit structure, although a map identifies its location on the grounds.

San Ignacio de Cabórica

Kino initially visited this mission site, colloquially called San Ignacio, in 1687. In 1690 Luis María Pineli, SJ, was assigned and remained for three years until Father Campos, Kino's frequent traveling companion, replaced him. During the Pima uprising of 1695, Campos escaped harm, but houses, storerooms, and his clothing were burned. Incredibly, he remained at San Ignacio for forty-two years, directing the building, repair, and rebuilding of the facility that had been continually destroyed during Apache raids. By 1730 the church had markedly deteriorated because of neglect, probably because Campos's health had failed and he could not go on with his work. In 1737 he was removed from his post and died in July of that year en route to the Jesuit college in Chihuahua, Mexico. Gaspar Stiger, SJ, replaced him and remained at San Ignacio until his death in 1766. He was succeeded by Father Pauer, who was also at Guévavi doing double duty until the Jesuit expulsion in 1767. In 1768 San Ignacio became a cabecera under the Franciscans. Four years later, in 1772 the friar, Francisco Sánchez Zúñiga, OFM, was in residence and supervised major alterations, creating a well-furnished Franciscan church with three altars and a priest's residence out of a ruined Jesuit church.

Santa María Magdalena

Known familiarly as Magdalena, and famous for being Kino's final resting place, this visita of San Ignacio was his personal headquarters beginning about 1690 until he died in 1711. Campos supervised a building program that had begun in 1705, but both the church and a chapel were subsequently destroyed. A new mission complex was erected by 1730 but forty years later was in ruins. In November 1776, Apache, Seri, and Pima

FIGURE 5 ∾ Mission San Ignacio (near Magdalena). Photo by Fr. Charles
Polzer, SJ. Courtesy of the Arizona Historical Society, Tucson,
AHS# 28968.

Indians attacked again. The resident friar, Pedro Font, OFM, wrote that
the raiders set afire the roof over five of the seven rooms of his house,
broke into the church, "carried off the vestments, spilled the holy oils,
ripped the linens from the statues . . . ruined the baptismal font and
candlesticks."[58] While the chapel in which Kino was originally buried
has disappeared, his remains are preserved at the site.

San Pedro y San Pablo de Tubutama

Founded by Kino, Tubutama served as the general Jesuit headquarters with visitas at Santa Teresa, Atil, Oquitoa, and possibly the presidial church in Altar.[59] Forty-two families, twenty-two widows, and
twenty-five orphans lived here. The first mission building might have
been destroyed in an earlier Pima uprising of March 1695, but the records
are unclear. It is known, however, that the missionary in residence,

Daniel Januske, SJ, was away from his post during that assault and so his life was spared. The chapel and the house were burned and religious images, pictures, and vestments destroyed. A second adobe church was completed in 1699 and a third possibly in 1706. The mission had visitas at Santa Teresa, Atil, and Oquitoa at the time. Two more churches were built, with one containing more than fifty thousand adobes, each handmade individually by mission Indians. The church was burned in the 1751 revolt when Jacobo Sedelmayr, SJ, then the head of the Jesuit province in the Pimería Alta, was in charge. Father Sedelmayr was discouraged by the Indians' materialism and the need for bribery to interest them in Christianity. He wrote, "When they [the Indians] say they want to be Christians . . . it usually means they want a horse, clothing, knife, or cloth."[60] Afterward, Father Sedelmayr's successor, Luis Vivas, SJ, supervised the Indians who were building a new church, completed by 1764, with two altars, a small side chapel, and a sacristy. Recoiling

FIGURE 6 ❧ Photo of Mission Tubutama. Courtesy of the Arizona Historical Society, Tucson, AHS# 57696.

from Apache attacks, Antonio Barbastro, OFM, supervised the building of another church in the 1780s.

Tubutama ultimately became a planned settlement with houses surrounding a plaza and gates built into the walls for protection against marauding Indians. The gates were closed at night to protect the residents and their livestock. Father Barbastro wrote, "The people and their cattle did not leave the village until the sun was quite high and the whole mission had been fortified."[61]

Santa María de los Pimas Suamca

Father Kino celebrated the first mass here in November 1697, when it was the village of Pima Bugota. He and his military companion, Juan Mateo Manje, rested here until December 6, impressed by the generosity and agricultural achievements of its two hundred natives. The indigenes built its first church in 1706, but it was destroyed, possibly by Apaches, in 1730 and rebuilt the same year under the supervision of Father Keller on the site of the modern Sonoran village of Santa Cruz. Suamca functioned as a cabecera in 1746 with Cocóspera as its visita. In 1768 the Apaches attacked Suamca, newly under Franciscan administration. The priest, Francisco Roche, OFM, transferred everyone to Cocóspera, and the mission remained abandoned until 1787.

౨

Writing in 1764 about the effects of Apache raiding on these and other missions, Juan Nentvig, SJ, noted that, despite the large numbers of livestock that had been sent from Mexico City to Sonora, there was often a lack of sufficient cattle, oxen, mules, and horses at the facilities because of the constant attacks. "The shortage is so acute," he noted, "that residents do not have enough beef to slaughter or saddle animals to ride in quest of sustenance for their families." He cautioned that the deficiency should be blamed

> on the prowling of Apaches and the Seris. One needs only to look at the 300 nearly abandoned ranches . . . that have lost more than 4000 mules, mares, and horses in the last seven years to realize this is true . . . It is God's merciful design that the Apache scatter their forces over a large area and do not as a unit

attack us, for there could be no place within the entire province that could be held against a united Apache effort. The whole province could be destroyed within a year . . ."[62]

Typically there was no discernible pattern to Apache assaults, no way the always vulnerable Europeans could predict the raids, no way they could prevent them. When the captured Apaches were incarcerated at the missions, these religious facilities took on the air of prison camps, but still the priests eagerly attempted to indoctrinate the Apaches into Christianity, an effort that would be mostly futile. Successful conversion to Christianity was often elusive among many Indian groups. Father Polzer believed that hardly any mission ever accomplished the formidable task of converting all the Indians within its jurisdiction and once the mission itself was firmly established and functioning, less attention was paid to the holdouts than might have been expected.[63]

A different type of violence was also part of daily life in the missions: contagious diseases that thrived unrestrained in the bones and blood of the indigenes who literally had no immunity. Hundreds of thousands of mission Indians and others still free perished over time. Lay persons and missionaries unsuccessfully treated ailments with prayers and the uses of natural remedies they learned from the Indians, but most were ineffective against the strange sicknesses the Europeans brought.[64] Epidemics raced across the frontier like wildfires.[65] As the traveling missionaries arrived at visitas they often found many Indians close to death. So many died that the priests deliberately designed a plan to replace the declining mission populations, one that oddly but pragmatically accepted the polygamous practices many tribes practiced.

"Marriage customs among the various northern tribes differed among themselves, and all of them were at variance with the monogamous practice of the Roman Catholic Church," reported Father Polzer. "The methodology regarding marriage [among the mission Indians] did not involve a harsh insistence on strict monogamy, but a staunch persuasion on the value of a firm union, contracted as a consenting adult."[66] In other words, by permitting a loosening of the orthodoxy regarding monogamous relationships among the mission Indians, the Jesuits hoped to attract more natives who, in turn, would increase the census, replenish the workforce, possibly procreate, and adopt Christianity.

With monogamy as the only exception, the Jesuits held firm on the other standards of Roman Catholic behavior. They stressed confession, for example, teaching that it was the proper way to enumerate sins. "The Indians generally kept track of their sins on small knotted cords," Father Polzer reported, "which they presented to the Father in confession . . . In the beginning the Indians were instructed to tell the Father that they did not wish to omit any sins, so they handed over the whole cord. With the priest's absolution, they understood they were free of all their sins."[67]

Confession and its connection to sins were confusing and troubling to the future converts since many indigenes had no traditional frame of reference to understand the idea of sin. They recognized bad judgment, yes, but did the Indians equate that with sin? Probably not, according to Kidwell, who wrote that the Indian peoples lacked "specific terms for such concepts as sin, guilt and salvation" in their languages and that made it difficult if not impossible for the missionaries to convey some of the basic tenets of Roman Catholicism.[68]

Still, erratic progress toward the clergy's dual goals of conversion and acculturation appeared unstoppable. Through examples and lessons the Jesuits taught the mission Indians how to farm, manage the range, and handle the livestock. Horses, mares, colts, stallions, brood mares, mules, and donkeys feasted on the wild grasses that covered much of the countryside. The natural reproduction of these domesticated healthy animals was so high that in time thousands roamed freely and mingled with wild animals in the open ranges near the missions.

The abundance of natural resources, the intelligent application of animal management techniques, and agricultural proficiency formed the foundations of a mission's subsistence economy that, in turn, could not have occurred without the Europeans' reliance on unpaid, forced Indian labor. When ready, all the mission products were processed, stocked, or traded, so that eventually the Jesuits operated on the colonial frontier as a principal producer and provider for the presidios' military personnel, in direct competition with the civilian ranchers and farmers. Together with overseeing and participating in these functions, the priests contin-ued proselytizing and evangelizing the Indians within and without the boundaries of the missions when possible.

In 1767 the Jesuits came under attack by Carlos III, who unexpect-edly expelled them from their Pimería Alta posts. His decree read in part,

"Because of weighty considerations which His Majesty keeps hidden in his heart, the entire Society of Jesus and all the Jesuits must leave the country and their establishments and properties must be turned over to the royal Treasurer. February 27, 1767."[69]

The official notice of removal was received in Mexico City on June 25. A month later, on July 23, Gov. Juan Claudio de Pineda of the Mexican states of Sonora and Sinaloa, assisted by a well-known military leader, Capt. Bernardo de Urrea, enforced the instruction. Two days later, fifty-two Jesuits met in the chapel of San José de Matape, Sonora. The church was ringed with barriers, and soldiers aimed their guns through the windows at the priests. At the end of the reading of the order for removal, the Jesuits marched under armed guard to the seacoast town of Guaymas where they lingered for eight months. After a series of travels, they boarded the final boat and sailed for Europe in April of 1769; twenty were dead by the time they arrived. The survivors lived out their lives scattered across Spain in jails and monasteries. Some were persecuted.

During more than 150 years on the colonial frontier, the Jesuits introduced Christianity and demonstrated the benefits of the Spanish culture to many natives. Under Jesuit tutelage, many Indians first heard the word of God, practiced the Roman Catholic faith, and learned the European culture. Many became literate, could farm, and run livestock. Regardless of their illegal and immoral actions, the Jesuits were successful in convincing many indigenes to participate in the wonder and glory of Christianity, as they saw and practiced it. The legacy is alive today.

Comments of the late Charles Polzer, SJ

"The Jesuits [on the Spanish colonial frontier] were always alone. Every man was a single man wherever he was, and he kept in contact by correspondence and other forms of communication, but not by living together. So, you find a networking among the Jesuits . . . It's a significant difference between the Jesuits and the Franciscans [where] two or three people would live together in a tiny community.

"Therefore that meant that the Jesuit was not going to be obligated to get together with his companions to pray the office, the hours, which the Society essentially doesn't do. A Jesuit [rose] early and . . . said mass in the morning because you had to fast . . . You had to approach that with full fast and abstinence. Indians were always invited in to pray and celebrate at that morning mass. Not everybody came. A lot of women came, but the men would go out to work in the fields or tend their horses . . . they were not expected to be there. In the morning the kids in the mission village would be given lessons, sometimes depending on the catechism and exercises. There would be a stress on music, a lot of emphasis on musical instrument training. Then mathematics and Spanish were taught.

"The day had a regular prayer life to it. The missionary directed community prayers, did the education and other work as well. At night he usually wrote letters, books, or kept up the mission books. The only thing that would vary the routine would be a feast day. These were almost all centered on liturgical days on the calendar. In preparation they did a lot of teaching morality plays. They were very, very strong on music [but dance] was looked upon as being pagan, but of course it makes very little difference . . . The motif has been transformed into something that is more in line with Christian liturgy, in the sense that they are honoring the Virgin or the Holy Spirit."[70]

౼

The Franciscans

During the year between 1767 and 1768, the colonial frontier was filled with politically appointed civil commissioners whose task was to evaluate and retrieve, if possible, any valuable Jesuit remainders. Joseph Och, SJ, wrote that these officials searched "every corner [of a mission] in vain. Practically all the bricks were torn loose from the floor . . . the garden was dug up . . . Walls were tapped inside and out and as soon as the sound seemed to reveal a space, it was broken in, but no sealed coin repositories were found."[71] This activity was no doubt fueled by false rumors throughout the Pimería Alta describing the riches in gold the Jesuits left behind. One wonders about the Indians' reactions to this looting. Did they participate? Observe?

One year later, in 1768, the viceroy of New Spain, Antonio Bucareli, expressed his concern that spiritual and material benefits to the empire were being lost because there were no missionaries in northwestern areas of the viceroyalty. As a result, fourteen friars from the Franciscan college in Querétaro, Mexico, under the leadership of Father Pres. Antonio Buena y Alcalde, replaced the Jesuits and were assigned to eight missions.[72] Also awaiting the missionaries were "16 villages, 2018 Indians, 179 civilized people, soldiers and their families, a total of 6489 souls. There were thousands of 'free' Indians as well."[73] Only a small number of Indians had stayed at or near abandoned missions with no supervision.

The Most Rev. J. B. Salpointe, DD, described the day the friars left for northern Sonora. "On the 5th of August [1768], which had been appointed for the start of the missionaries, all the community assembled in the chapel, as we read in the *Cronica Serafica* where, after the adoration of the Blessed Sacrament, the 'Tota Polchra as Maria,' or 'Thou art all beautiful, O Mary,' was sung to implore the protection of the mother of God for the new apostles and their missions. These priests, having embraced their brothers in religion and recommended themselves to their prayers, set out on their journey."[74]

Charles R. Carlisle and Bernard Fontana reported that upon arriving in northern Mexico, the Franciscans'

> overall impression [of their new environment was] of poverty-stricken missions located on cold, wind-swept mesas and mountains, plagued by a scarcity of water and wood, with a population almost entirely Indian which lacked the devout zeal which the missionaries greatly desired—conditions which made it impossible for the churches to support themselves as parishes.[75]

No longer evident at some missions were livestock, farm equipment, and the surplus produce from the earth. Either the civil commissioners had raided the Jesuit storerooms, or the Indians had torn up the fields. At a few sites, only portions of the mission buildings themselves remained, either having been burned or destroyed during the one-year hiatus.

In the words of Father Alcalde, "The ones [missions] that have been given to us are the least populous, the poorest and most painful, located in the only unhealthful climate in all these vast provinces." After observing the indigenes, he wrote that they live "in perpetual idleness, wandering the backcountry from one mission to another . . . We cannot reprimand them . . ."[76] It appears that the Franciscans had not yet applied the concept of bribery; it would come later to influence the natives some friars described as "crude, lazy, shameless, irresponsible, ill-disciplined Christians in name only."[77]

With very little support, the Franciscans were expected to repair and rebuild the damage to the buildings, manage the religious aspect of the missions, convert the non-Christian Indians, feed themselves and the natives, and get along only on a small annual stipend of 360 pesos for each priest. Added to the friars' distress was the fact that their activities were limited to the spiritual only; they were prohibited from any other activity such as selling agricultural produce for profit. Agents of the government were appointed to manage mission businesses, ensuring that the crown would realize substantial profits from the sale of products produced through the indigenes' forced labor. If interference in any grand plans was unwelcome news to the Franciscans, there was more to come. An eight-point set of instructions from their Franciscan superiors directed the friars to observe the following:

1) Treat the Indians with paternal love;
2) Suggest means of expanding mission to include nonbelievers;
3) Submit reports containing a few negative remarks only;
4) Allow civil interactions between Indians and Spaniards;
5) Encourage the Indians to become self-sufficient;
6) Teach the Indians how to speak Spanish and sponsor a school in each mission;
7) Inventory the furnishings, making certain that baptismal, marriage, and burial books were in order and conduct a detailed census of mission residents; and
8) Exercise the ecclesiastical faculties.[78]

While some of these guidelines gave the natives more freedom and opportunity, they clearly limited the Franciscans' control and their ability to evangelize. For example, if the Indians left the mission area to resume hunting and gathering in the hinterlands (condition number 5), there might be very few neophytes remaining in the immediate surroundings to hear the Word of God. Worse, the indigenes might not return at all. Between 1767 and 1768 the mission Indians had been free from religious supervision and instruction, and many surely had returned to a traditional life-style. Salpointe wrote, "There were many among them who were considered to be Christians because they had been baptized, but who knew more of deviltry than of Catholic doctrine."[79]

The friars were distressed but characteristically compliant and, despite disappointments, began to establish a routine at the missions. Their patience was rewarded after one year, for in 1769 they received control of all the facets—religious and secular—of the missions when the business managers were suddenly relieved of their duties.

After a few weeks of following the eight-point plan, Alcalde wrote that "only the Indians who feel like it come to catechism, without according us so far even the slightest recognition or more attention than a stranger might get in their pueblo."[80] Despite these misgivings, the devoted Franciscans applied themselves to the myriad of tasks that presented themselves at their assigned missions, now including convincing Indians to remain and others to return.

Los Santos Ángeles de Guévavi

Juan Gil de Bernabé, OFM, took charge of this easternmost cabecera with visitas at San Ignacio de Sonoitac, San José de Tumacácori, and San Cayetano de Calabazas. In late 1769 Apaches attacked Guévavi despite a wall for protection that the Indians under Franciscan supervision had recently built. Gil de Bernabé remained in charge of Guévavi for four years, leaving in the spring of 1772 to begin a Seri Indian mission at Carrizal. Seris murdered him there on March 7, 1773. Francisco Zúñiga, OFM, an interim priest, helped Gil de Bernabé during the latter part of his tenure but was transferred to San Ignacio by January 1772. In the summer of 1772, Bartholomé Ximeno, OFM, took charge of Guévavi where he remained for one year before being transferred to Tumacácori. Nineteen families initially lived at Guévavi under early Franciscan supervision, as did five widowers, seven widows, and twelve orphans, for a total of eighty-six persons. Three years later there were "only nine families living at Guevavi."[81] Guévavi was abandoned in 1776 because of continuing Apache attacks. Its functions, and Father Ximeno, were moved to Tumacácori. Toward the end of that year, Gaspar Clemente, OFM, joined Father Ximeno at Tumacácori.

Tumacácori was located in a very fertile region on the west bank of the Santa Cruz River. Walls around the compound had been erected,

FIGURES 7 AND 8 ❧ "Ruins of Guévavi mission." Photos by author.

and a church and a priest's house were available, but the home was unfurnished. Mission Indians had built a few adobe houses. Ninety-three people lived at Tumacácori, twenty-two families, twelve widowers, and ten orphans in 1784.

The visita of San Ignacio de Sonoitac offered both a church and a house to a missionary, but the home had no furniture. Eighteen families, twenty widowers and single men, and twelve widows, for a total of ninety-four Pimas, lived at Sonoitac.

Calabazas appeared favorable for farming, but the Indians cultivated little or no land. Father Ximeno complained that the residents had to travel too far from their homes to work the farmland. Under constant threat of Apache attacks, the people had to take all their possessions with them whenever they left Calabazas. "They even carry their chickens and all their meager furniture from their little houses to work with them," quoted Don Garate. "It is at those sites that the Apaches frequently fall upon the people and the only sanctuary the poor unfortunates have is to seek shelter in the neighboring woods and hide themselves there."[82] By the end of the 1780s, the residents of Calabazas had been assimilated into the mission at Tumacácori. Seventeen families, four widowers, and seven widows, for a total of sixty-four persons, had lived here at the beginning of the Franciscan administration in 1768.

San Xavier del Bac

Francisco Garces, OFM, took charge of this northern cabecera. He wrote a letter dated July 29, 1768, to Comm. Juan Bautista de Anza, away temporarily from his troops at the neighboring Tubac presidio, after he had been shown hospitality by Anza's family. In part the letter read, "As for myself, I am very happy here. I was warned of the hardships that awaited me, but so far these have consisted of but a few flies and mosquitoes. I am told that the Jesuit fathers found it very difficult to subsist here, even with their cattle, horses, and fields. Armed only with my royal stipend, which they had as well, I have not found it so."[83] Pima Indians who remained at the mission during the one-year absence of supervision had raised hundreds of acres of wheat and corn in the surrounding fields, an inviting circumstance for friends and relatives who thought about coming back. At the close of 1771, two years after Garces's arrival (he remained until 1778), forty-eight families lived at Bac, along with

FIGURE 9 ∾ "Juan Bautista de Anza." Drawing by José Cisneros. From Kieran
McCarty, OFM, *Desert Documentary: The Spanish Years, 1767–1821*
(Tucson: Arizona Historical Society, 1976).

seven widowers, twelve widows, and twenty-six orphans, for a total community of 170 persons.

The visita of San José de Tucson, nine miles north, had neither a church nor a dwelling for a missionary in 1769 although the population was estimated at more than two hundred heads of families, Christian and Indian. Under Garces's direction, a church, a house for him and any other friar who would follow, and a wall for defense against Apache attacks were built.[84]

San Ignacio de Cabórica

Diego Martín García, OFM, led this cabecera and its visitas of San José de Imuris and Santa María Magdalena. San Ignacio's church had three altars, the sacristy was well furnished, and a house adjoined the church. Mission Indians cultivated wheat, corn, and beans. Thirty-six families lived here, as did seven widows and four widowers, for a total of 148 people. García also took care of fifteen orphans.

Excavations in 1935 unearthed a cemetery east of the church, once surrounded by a wall seven feet high and twenty-one inches thick. A few niches in the wall interrupted the smooth flow of adobe bricks; these walls might have held skulls, a common custom of the time.[85]

Apache attacks ruined most of the visita of Magdalena; only the chapel remained in fair condition. The sacristy held a chalice and a few old altar ornaments, along with some furniture. Nineteen families, five widowers, one widow, and six orphans, in all thirty-nine persons, lived in the area.

San Padro y San Pablo de Tubutama

Father Alcalde, the leader of the Franciscans, administered the mission and made it his headquarters. In 1768 Tubutama was flourishing. The missionary's house was spacious, the garden was well tended, and the 176 people living at the mission—forty-five families, twelve widowers, six widows, and eighteen orphans—raised wheat, corn, and beans. The church's sacristy contained three chalices and all the material required for mass. Apaches murdered Felipe Guillén, OFM, a priest at Tubutama from 1774 to 1778, as he traveled from the visita at Santa Teresa whose church was bare of any ornaments, as was the house for the priest. The Indian population was thirteen families, seven widowers and single men, and two widows, for a total of fifty-two persons.

Santa María de los Pimas Suamca

Francisco Roche, OFM, was in charge of the cabecera with responsibilities at the visita of Nuestra Senõra del Pilar y Santiago de Cocóspera. An Apache attack destroyed Suamca's church and mission in late 1768. Roche and a few Indian men, women, and children fled to Cocóspera, but Apaches leveled that site too during the same year. A few unsuccessful attempts were made to rebuild the main mission, but as of 1784 Suamca was still unoccupied. The total population of the cabecera and visita did not at any time exceed 110 people, which, in 1768, included thirty families, five widowers, and twenty widows.

❧

The wealth or poverty of each mission varied all across the frontier, influenced by the priests' management skills; the quality of the soil; the quantity of Indian attacks; and the cooperation, ambition, or resistance of the neophytes. For control, and to force order through regimentation, the friars planned each day at the missions to be as similar as possible to the previous one. For example, after morning religious services, Indian laborers involuntarily walked to their fields to work all day at planting and raising wheat, corn, and melons. The field workers knew that no matter how hard they labored each day, they would have to wait for harvest time when they could take the amount of crops they needed for themselves and their families out of the surplus storage area. Until then the extra crops, if any, were stored to eventually be used for the good of the community or sold to the presidios and growing number of settlers. Periodic Apache attacks resulting in abandonment of secular settlements and villages so devastated many missions' economies, however, that the facilities frequently had no market for their agricultural produce. Nonetheless, the Indians continued to be assigned to the fields for a long day's labor.

The friars' added concern regarding the workforce was that some Indians were more energetic than others, some less. As the healthy Indians' stamina was dedicated to producing food, continuing the religious, educational, and building programs became secondary. More and more returning families were immediately put to work to repair the fields that had been inactive for a year. Much of the vast acreage needed weeding, the soil had to be turned, and the crops had to be replanted.

Debris-cluttered irrigation channels had to be cleaned out and, in several cases, redug. At sunset each day the tired workers walked far distances back to the villages and, before food was eaten, were required to stop at the mission to say the "the Doctrina and prayers . . . in the plaza in front of the church," reported Bernard Fontana, in an effort to reintroduce Christian concepts.[86]

Other problems surfaced immediately. Like the Jesuits, the Franciscans had difficulties with the language differences, but "the missionaries used their good sense," wrote Zephryin Englehardt. "They instructed the savages in the vernacular as soon as they had acquired sufficient knowledge to make themselves understood."[87] Absent the "good sense," it would have been easier for the friars than for the Jesuits to communicate with the Indians because most of the mission Indians had already learned some Spanish.

Eager Franciscans pursued every opportunity to baptize, often without the parents' full understanding of the meaning of the sacrament, and then recorded the new "Christian's" name in ledgers just as the Jesuits had done. During these deeply religious ceremonies, the priest often gave his own name to the Indian child. "Thus we find [a child named] Francisco Hermenegildo Herran, who was almost certainly baptized by Father Francisco Hermenegildo Garces," wrote Alfred Whiting, also noting that

> Francisco Nuñez, born in 1770 may well have been baptized by Father Francisco Zuniga when he called at Tumacacori in 1771 . . . Similarly, Juan Chrisostomos Zuniga (born about 1770) was probably named by Father Juan Chrisostomos Gil de Bernabe who was at Guevavi from 1768 to 1772 . . . Judging from birth dates, such names came into use only after the coming of the Franciscans . . . The Jesuits . . . rarely recorded a family name for any Indian.[88]

While that may be true, some Jesuits viewed naming a bit differently, uniquely one could say. Kessell wrote about Father Keller, who visited Pima rancherias in 1737, "where he had baptized twenty-six females, bestowing on all of them the name Catalina 'in order to avoid confusion.' For the same reason, and with a keen sense of proportion, he left behind him as well twenty-six new Ignacios."[89]

In the Franciscans' eyes, baptisms ensured the children a place in heaven, an important consideration because of everyone's extreme vulnerability to the continuing danger from Apache attacks and contagious diseases. The young, the old, the already ailing, and the undernourished indigenes were still defenseless against the many ailments that were easily spread from person to person. As one exception, however, no one, not even the Europeans, was exempt from the ravages of syphilis, brought to New Spain in the bodies of the newcomers and soon visited upon the Indians. Unfortunately, the literature is silent on the effects of sexually transmitted diseases on northern Mexico's indigenous women.

The deaths of young, strong Indian men from communicable diseases placed a noticeable drain on the rebuilding programs. Most important, sick or dying women of childbearing age could not reproduce children who would be added to the baptism rolls and, through those numbers, bring in more supplies, livestock, and items needed to keep the mission afloat. Kessell wrote that the "declining Indian population always vexed the missionaries."[90]

Because of large numbers of deaths, the population of Indians to be indoctrinated into Christianity declined during the Franciscan era and caused an adverse impact on reported statistics that, in turn, demonstrated to far-off authorities in Mexico City who interpreted them, the Franciscans' lack of success in religious conversion. With a drop in the recorded number of souls saved, government or church officials could decide to partially or totally amend their support of the missions, usually by reducing rations or other benefits. This they did, just as they had done in the Jesuit era.

A discussion of colonial frontier ailments must include the consequences of the chronic diseases that did not kill as rapidly but decimated the Indians. Their gastrointestinal tracts were strangers to the European diet and foodstuffs such as white flour, sugar, pork, chicken, sheep, and chocolate. Horsemeat and beef caused bowel distress, especially among infants who were often afflicted with deadly dysentery. Among adults, debilitating diarrhea, while not always fatal, certainly interrupted an individual's ability to work at agricultural or construction tasks and concentrate and fill the obligations the new religion imposed.

Vulnerable priests also fell ill, and Father Englehardt reported that in a period of eleven years, "six new fathers arrived to take the place of deceased or infirm missionaries" at the eight missions.[91] Replacements were not always completely immune to the chronic or contagious diseases, and some of the substitute friars also had to be taken off duty. Caywood reported that between the years 1768 and 1836, there were sixty-one Franciscan priests in northern Sonora.[92] Whether these were visitors, temporary stand-ins because of others' incapacities, or friars actually assigned to the missions is unclear.

Climatic conditions also increased the number of ailing individuals and fatalities. Warm winter weather in Sonora was conducive to the spread of contagion, especially among those living in close proximity, as mission Indians did. Another condition to be considered is the amount of food an individual received. When supplies were adequate, nourishment had a positive effect on general health and resulted in varying degrees of resistance to disease. At some missions the Indians supplemented their sparse diet through traditional hunting and gathering methods, at others this was not permitted.

Against this difficult background the frontier Franciscans continued to introduce the concepts and practice of Christianity to the natives. One of each missionary's essential daily duties was to "count the people in the morning, preach to them, and sing Mass, baptize both children and adults, confess the sick, and bury the dead." In addition the friars taught religious lessons that focused on "bowing the head, kneeling, maintaining a hushed silence, and stillness in the manner of Spanish piety. Four main prayers were taught by rote."[93]

None of this impressed the Apaches, who continued to raid and kill. The situation became so overwhelming that on August 26, 1786, Carlos III appointed Bernardo de Gálvez as viceroy of New Spain and charged him with reviewing the disastrous situation. His efforts resulted in a document known as the Instructions of 1786 that contained three main objectives to subdue the Chiricahuas:

1) Exploit discord among them and form alliances with other Indians against them, with the goal of causing the natives to destroy each other;

2) Continue to wage constant warfare against them up to the point of exterminating them if necessary; and

3) Offer peace terms to those Apaches who asked for them and, after

determining their intentions were sincere, reward them with amenities designed to foster dependence.[94]

In order to receive the above benefits, however, the Apaches would have to leave their camps, relocate at or near the presidios or missions in what came to be called "peace establishments" placed all across the frontier, and subject themselves to Spanish supervision. The Franciscans decided the Jesuits had the right idea: once again bribery was expected to lead to Christianization.

The missions' original purposes of conversion and assimilation were, for the most part, now eclipsed by the emphasis on the military provisions of the policy, but the friars were nonetheless expected to continue proselytizing the native groups and play a major role in Christianizing the Chiricahua Apaches—those who were about to voluntarily surrender, those who had been captured and were already living in the missions, and those who would be seized and imprisoned in the near future.

Comments of Kieran McCarty, OFM

"Spanish policy [operated] under the assumption that the Franciscans were enlightened and had a higher morality than just about anyone else . . . the problem, though, was concepts. The Indian often couldn't understand what we were saying. They didn't have the words to understand Father, Son, and Holy Spirit.

"The Franciscans were the good guys and had a tradition of hospitality and kindness. I don't mean that the Jesuits wore the black hats, but they operated in the age of power. They came like visiting wise men to northern New Spain. They had a very religious ethos and still do, but some of the Spanish Jesuits had a strict, domineering attitude toward the natives. On the other hand, there were delightful Franciscans. Today, St. Francis is still universally loved. A kinder man there never was."[95]

Tubac, Tumacácori, Janos, and Cuba

⅗ SAN IGNACIO DE TUBAC, A SMALL BUT MIGHTY PRESIDIO THAT WAS established after the 1751 Pima revolt, had one major purpose: protecting the Spanish settlers in the area and the cabecera of Guévavi and its visitas, including Tumacácori. This frequently deadly assignment was part of the process of bringing this vast land and its indigenous peoples under Spanish control; success was often elusive.

One excellent example of the effort native groups expended to resist the Spanish occupation was the Pima revolt itself that began during the night of November 20–21, 1751, at the Pima village of Sáric, when Indian leader Luis Oacpicagigua's diligently planned, secret rebellion against the Spanish occupation burst out. Luis and his followers had been allied with the Spaniards against the more warlike tribes in the area, but after the Jesuit, Ignacio Keller, upset about an infraction of the rules, made the mistake of humiliating Luis in public, the Indian's attitude changed dramatically.[1] Luis's slowly festering plans of rebellion suddenly ripened, and loyal messengers carried word to the other participating indigenous settlements. At the agreed-upon day many furious strikes against the occupiers bloodied the frontier.[2]

The Pima village of Tchoowaka (Tubac) was attacked but missed a goodly portion of violence because of a stroke of good luck.[3] One of the raiders recognized his godmother, it is said, and dissuaded his marauding companions from laying waste to the entire settlement. Most of the startled villagers abandoned their homes and quickly escaped to the north. Left behind for unknown reasons were a resident named Pasqual,

FIGURE 10 ∞ "Photo of a pencil sketch by John Ross Browne in 1869, Tubac, Arizona. Company E volunteers provided labor for adobe blocks used in buildings of the Fort." From *The Smoke Signal* 67 (Spring 1997).

a female relative, and child. When it was safe, soldiers from Terranate, a fort not too distant from the action, arrived. They allowed the three frightened people to ride into the mountains, find any relatives and friends, and convince them to return.[4]

One month later, at least forty former residents wandered back in time for spring planting,[5] although Henry Dobyns reported that within the next ten years many Pimas left this village, moved to nearby Tumacácori, and settled there.[6] Not mentioned was the possibility that many of the indigenes were forced to relocate by soldiers who had another agenda—land usurpation.

Only three miles down the road from the presidio at Tubac, a Sobaípuri village called Tumacácori had been established for more than one hundred years on the east bank of what became the Santa Cruz River.[7] Early Jesuits had already proselytized the indigenous settlement before the venerable Eusebio Kino's first visit in 1691, as shown by three ramadas prepared in advance for him—one under which he would say mass, another to protect him during his sleep, and a third for cooking. Forty huts in which the natives lived were nearby.[8] In his future travels, Father Kino stopped at Tumacácori several times. During one visit in particular, on November 26, 1697, he arrived with his military escort, Juan Mateo Manje. Captain Manje wrote of that visit, stating there were 150 souls who greeted them with dances and songs. In anticipation of this visit, the Indians had built Father Kino another more elaborate adobe house with a main room and living quarters; Father Kino baptized one child on that day with officer Manje serving as the godparent.[9]

For years the fertile valley on both sides of the Santa Cruz River had lured Spanish newcomers with interests in farming and ranching, despite the frequent threat of danger from Indian raids and increasing deadly assaults. These attacks and the anxiety they generated underscored the need for a garrisoned fort, so ordinary citizens and well-connected ranchers made their requests known to Spanish authorities. After much bureaucratic wrangling that followed the Pima revolt of 1751, in late 1752 officials agreed to the proposal and the Real Presidio de San Ignacio de Tubac became a reality. Located approximately on the site of Tchoowaka, the presidio's first captain was Juan Tomás Beldarrain; he remained in that position until his death on September 7, 1759.[10] Using volunteer soldiers and the Indians' forced labor, Beldarrain directed construction of the fortress during the years 1756–67. High walls with breaks around the parapet were specifically designed to enable gunners to poke their weapons through, fire, drop to their knees, and be protected from retaliation. Horses stood at the ready in a corral near the presidio just in case a sentry, peering through a break in the parapet, spied Apaches on the move. More than one hundred campaigns against the Apaches alone were recorded from 1752 to 1776.[11]

ᴄ⅋

In the one year between the Jesuit removal in 1767 and the Franciscan presence on the frontier in 1768, Tubac's presidial soldiers became sloppy and undisciplined. Recognizing this, the Apaches mocked them, taunted them, and screamed at them during the military's excursions into Apache territory. Despite the anticipated rewards combat would bring, many soldiers lost heart and courage, deserting their stations, while others simply refused to fight. New recruits seldom stayed long, many fleeing in terror

MAP 2 ≈ "The Pimería Alta of Father Kino." From Charles W. Polzer, SJ, *Kino: A Legacy* (Tucson: Jesuit Fathers of Arizona, 1998).

after their first experience with the Chiricahuas, who had begun raiding as soon as the Franciscans reconstituted the missions.

Here too, as it was during the Jesuit era, killing mission residents in any of those raids seemed almost accidental, a fact that has been noted by Maria Soledad Arbelaez who wrote, "An outstanding feature of . . . reports is the constant complaint raised . . . that the main reason for the Indian attacks was to pillage the mission's property . . . Total destruction was rarely the case since the Indians attacked symbols of domination, church buildings, crosses, and saints' images."[12]

As a pragmatic people, the Chiricahua Apaches reasoned that killing the newcomers was not an immediate option, for that would mean that the desirable supplies the Europeans brought to the frontier—livestock, tools, musical instruments, and so forth—would soon be exhausted and probably, in Apache thinking, not replaced. If the signs of the outsiders such as churches were attacked at first, though, perhaps they would leave the frontier. That approach made a lot of sense to the Chiricahuas; in today's vernacular it would be "sending them a message."

So the raiders ripped paintings from the church walls and furiously tore or cut the missals to pieces during attacks. Many oil canvases depicted valuable representations of sacred subjects and were unable to be repaired or restored on the frontier. The raiders poured holy oils on the ground, burned the priests' religious clothing, and threw wooden statues of various saints in fires. They smashed chalices and pulverized baptismal fonts. They set church roofs afire and attempted to raze the physical structures. Successful in some instances, it was not as a total result of their efforts because "the beams were rotten, the roof leaking, and the old adobes washing away," wrote Father McCarty.[13]

Each attack was carefully planned, characteristic of a raiding society. Before leaving the campsite the leader consulted with medicine men and medicine women who were empowered to predetermine the outcomes of most situations. If these seers declared that the time was right, the warriors attacked openly and unafraid, screaming in fury atop previously purloined Spanish horses, waving and firing pilfered Spanish guns, letting their presence be known in advance but usually not soon enough for an effective Spanish military reaction from a nearby presidio. There was no pattern to the raids on missions, no way the Europeans could predict the assaults or prevent them. Their best responses resulted in killing or capturing a number of Apaches and incarcerating them at the missions where the priests could begin indoctrination, or distributing them as slaves to military households.

In February and March 1776, for example, Tubac's military commander, Juan Bautista de Anza, led a combined force from several presidios, including Pima auxiliary scouts, into Apache country.[14] This particular foray resulted in several Apaches being killed and forty taken captive. According to the accepted procedures of the time, these captive men, women, and children could become slaves, distributed by lot among their captors: fifteen were women, some with newborn infants, and were Anza's personal share.[15] Zavala wrote, "Soldiers frequently went on expeditions into the Indian country . . . to capture slaves. These men, women, and children were sold . . . The minimum age for enslavements was ten and a half years for boys, nine and a half for girls; young captives were kept in temporary bondage up to the age of twenty . . . [Adults] were valued between two hundred and fifty and three hundred pesos each, and younger ones . . . from one hundred and fifty to two hundred pesos."[16] There is also evidence in parish baptismal records, William Griffen

FIGURE 11 ∽ "Cemetery at Tubac." Photo by author.

reported, in which "Apache were baptized, sometimes traded for a horse, a calf, or cash to a Spanish family that adopted the child."[17] Griffen's statement raises questions about who benefited from the trade. Were the priests the recipients of livestock or cash, or did the priests return the captives, after baptism, to the military for trade? Moreover, what did the word "adoption" infer? It is well known that families receiving Indian children were obliged to educate and instill Christian values in them, but whether this actually happened is questionable in many cases.

Anza then continued his march and found seventy Apaches camped atop a mountain near the present-day Arizona town of San Simon. His troop killed two and captured forty more. He returned to Tubac after three weeks in the field only because of an undiagnosed epidemic among his Indian scouts. Two had died, and he feared more deaths if he kept them in the field with little protection and great exertions.[18] Anza's decision to return to the presidio is confusing, as the sick scouts would bring the strange ailment into the presidio environment and other people would then fall ill. Anza's options were limited, though; he could not keep the ailing men on patrol.

In 1768 while Anza was in California—he had been temporarily transferred—his troops held the fort at Tubac and protected Tumacácori's mission. In December of that year, twenty-six soldiers and fifty Indian auxiliaries ventured into Apache country but encountered so many Apaches that they quickly retreated.[19]

In April 1769 Apaches attacked the Pimas guarding the mission of San Xavier del Bac and stole the animals. Tubac troops gave chase with ten soldiers, fifteen citizens, and forty Pimas. Sighting the Apaches north of the Gila River, the officer in charge quickly evaluated the situation, decided the Indians were too numerous to fight, and retreated.[20]

Back from California in late July or early August 1771, Anza and a column of thirty-four soldiers and fifty Pimas rode out of Tubac to hunt Apaches. On August 9 they discovered an Apache encampment on the banks of the upper Gila River, killed nine, took eight prisoners, and recovered one Spanish captive; a number of wounded Apaches escaped.[21]

After failing in many such battles, Anza became disappointed in the strategy under way to repel Apache attacks—defeat them in battle—and suggested a different approach. "As for the advancement of these heathens and of those previously reduced, I say that the surest way to attain the worthy goals expressed . . . is to destroy and reform as useless and prejudicial the system up to now observed in the missions," he wrote.[22] Anza had seen for himself that the then-current means of fighting Apaches had failed to deter their assaults, so he advocated restructuring the entire operation to produce a nonmilitary program that would attract and pacify the Apaches. Jesuits had tried this idea—bribery—and failed. Now, under Franciscan supervision, the notion was seen as having potential even though the friars had made negligible progress in assimilating and acculturating any combative Apaches since their 1768 arrival. Nonetheless, despite the respect Anza held in official military circles, his recommendation was ignored, and the Apache attacks continued.

Many worries, including the ever-present military insecurity, beset the Franciscans immediately. For example, concern for the safety of the missionaries was just one problem that worried Father Bartolomé Ximeno, the resident priest at Tumacácori in 1772. He wrote about the dismal poverty at the mission and the ineffectiveness of Tubac's presidial soldiers to defend his mission against Apache attacks. He stated he had seen many murders, robberies, and atrocities Apaches had committed in the area and firmly believed that the entire Pimería Alta was doomed unless the Apaches were contained.[23]

These fears meant nothing to the Apaches, and their intentions to rid their country of human contaminants went on almost unabated. In November 1776, at the end of early mass, a group of forty Apaches attacked Santa María Magdalena. Only four men had been left behind to protect the village while others were away working in the fields, a fact not lost on the raiders, who had probably observed the routine for days before the assault. Magdalena's residents hastily took refuge in the missionary's quarters. Before burning the church next to the priest's house, the Apaches entered the building and broke or desecrated everything they could find. As they left, they carried out vestments and altar vessels and threw torn missal pages to the winds. Not satisfied, they returned a short time later and set the missionary's dwelling afire. As the flames reached the still-huddled people, the priest asked all to make an act of fervent contrition. Just then troops from nearby San Ignacio arrived and drove away the raiders, but not before the Indians seized and rode away with a woman and two children.[24]

When the dedicated Franciscans showed no signs of abandoning

FIGURE 12 ∾ "Presidio at Tubac." Photo by author.

missions despite the attacks—some missions were now being actively reconstituted with Pimas, Pápagos, and Yuman-speaking residents— remorseless Apache warriors switched their emphasis from destroying missions to destroying the civilian settlements, sometimes whole towns. The burning, pillaging, and brutality continued day after day unabated.[25]

Records identify by name and position but not ethnicity some of those killed during selected Apache attacks. For example, on December 9, 1743, raiders struck the Divisadero Ranch in the San Luis valley, killed three children named Guitera, José Manuel, and Juan Antonio, and two women, Narcisa, the wife of the rancher, and María Manuela, the wife of Augustín María Bermudes. The Guitera children may have been slaves, as further identification was not listed. All were buried in the cemetery at Suamca.[26]

On November 14, 1746, an attack occurred at the Pima village of Hasohuvaibca. Four people died, including Salvador, the Indian governor, an ox driver named Nicolás, a man named Xavier el Soldado, and Bartolo O'otassava, the husband of Chepa, a survivor. All were buried at the pueblo of San Pedro.[27]

On July 27, 1763, two died at Buena Vista, again in the San Luis valley, including one soldier named Ventura and María Catalina Morales, the wife of Cristóval de Chamorro. He was buried in Buena Vista and she probably in the cemetery at Guévavi. Documents show she had resided in San Ignacio, Tubac, and Magdalena; she likely was a Pima Indian.[28]

On February 1, 1769, an attack on the Santa Ana horse range, twenty miles south of San Ignacio, claimed three lives, including one unmarried man who was a soldier named Ponciano, a child named Juan José Carrisosa, and Domingo Otero, the Pima husband of María Josefa Mendoza. All three were buried in the cemetery at Magdalena.[29]

On May 4, 1770, a battle at Calabazas killed seven people, including one orphan child named Isabel María who lived at the mission, a husband and wife named Rosa and Andrés, María the wife of Lorenzo, a widow also named María, a widower named Ignacio, and Ana María, an unmarried woman. "Because of the circumstances, they died without Sacraments," wrote Father Gil de Bernabé. "They were provided ecclesiastical burial in the cemetery of Guevavi."[30]

A major battle, this one at Sonoitac, occurred on July 13, 1770, when nineteen people were killed, including the village's governor and his wife, single men and women, husbands and wives, and eleven boys and girls. The deceased may have been indigenes, as they are listed by first name only. All were buried in the cemetery at Sonoitac.[31]

Apaches attacked Tumacácori and Sonoitac on July 1, 1771, killing five adults, including Juan Tushumsiba, the husband of a survivor named Lucía; Inés, the wife of a survivor named Ignacio; Rosa, the wife of a lieutenant named Antonio; Xavier, the foreman of the oxen; and José, the husband of Josefa María; she survived. All were buried at Sonoitac with the exception of José and Juan, who were interred in the cemetery at Tumacácori. No information explains why some were buried in one place, some in another.[32]

On July 14, 1772, Apaches raided Guévavi, killing two widows, Isabel, a native of San Xavier; and Catalina, a Pima from Tucson; and María the wife of Tomás, who was the governor of Guévavi at the time; Tomás survived. The listing of these deaths is accompanied by a note from Father Ximeno, the friar who identified the decedents. He buried the bodies in Guévavi.[33]

On October 31, 1784, Apaches killed two widowers, Eusebio Gómez, about thirty years old, and Andrés Peralta, about fifty years old, in the mountains above Tumacácori. One wonders if the men were away from their village gathering firewood, or what other circumstances would have taken them so far from safety. Baltasar Carillo, OFM, buried them the next day in Tumacácori's cemetery.[34]

On June 5, 1801, Apaches attacked Tumacácori and killed three males, all "outside the compound." Juan Antonio Crespo was a Pima Indian from Caborca who lived at Tumacácori and was married to María Gertrudis Brixio. Félix Hurtado, age fifteen, was the son of Francisco Hurtado and Juana de Dios Mesa. A note from Narciso Gutiérrez, OFM, stated that the boy's body could not be retrieved and brought into the compound until the next day because the Apaches were lying in wait. José María Paxarito, age twenty, was a Yaqui Indian also living at Tumacácori, the son of Ramón Pixarito and María Plancha Platas. The friar could only bury Crespo on the same day. Hurtado and Paxarito were buried the next day in Tumacácori's cemetery.[35] Soldiers arriving on June 6 chased the Apaches away.[36]

These records are silent regarding any captives the Apaches seized during these assaults; prisoners could be incorporated into the tribe, traded back to the Spaniards later on, or killed. For example, a soldier named Félix Guerra had been captured, probably in early 1778. The Apaches later signaled their willingness to trade Guerra and three Spanish children for three Indian women prisoners who had been held in the Janos, Mexico, presidio. Negotiations began when cavalry Lt. don Naciso de Tapia and several military personnel rode out of the fort to deal with Apache chieftains Nateniju, Pachatiju, and El Sordo. Agreements could not be reached. On February 8, two Apache women entered the Janos presidio, bringing with them an offer to renew the exchange. The women told the army personnel the Apaches would await them the next day in the mountains. Seventy-two soldiers, settlers, Opata Indian auxiliaries, and an Indian guide rode out to meet the Apaches and the exchange was apparently made successfully.[37]

More recently, Chiricahua Apache Kathleen Kanseah, now an elder on the Mescalero Apache Reservation in New Mexico, talked about her family history. "My mother was Spanish," said Kathleen, "but from what I hear, one of her ancestors was captured in Tularosa [New Mexico] by the Apaches . . . When they were enrolling people into the tribe, they asked my grandparents if they would enroll their children. I think there were five or six of them in the family at that time. From what I understand, it was an act of Congress to get them enrolled into the tribe because they had Spanish blood. My mother's family was raised with the Apaches. My mother spoke Indian fluently, and so did the rest of the family except Uncle Paul and Uncle Mike, my mother's brothers."[38]

It is understandable that members of the military could have been reluctant to engage the Apaches in battle, especially since the danger of death was so high and the wages so low. Annual pay for the captain was set at 600 pesos, 450 for the lieutenant, and 420 for the ensign. Enlisted men were paid 400 pesos. Each trooper received a complete outfit of arms, body armor, saddle, bridle, and other horse gear, six good horses, and a uniform. All the equipment, including the horses, was charged to the soldier, however, who was expected to pay off his debt within the first year of service.[39] Given the perilous conditions of warfare inherent in encountering hostile Indians, the desertion rate among the troops was high, regardless of the benefits.

Officers and enlisted men received bonuses outside of their payment for services: public honor and the spoils of war that included "rights to the land, tax exemptions, rights to booty captured from defeated indigenes ... [and] cash payments given ... for Apache scalps and prisoners," wrote Ana Maria Alonso. Apache captives were distributed to officers as domestic servants.[40] This windfall flew in the face of the Reglamento of 1729, a law that specifically forbid Indian captives being assigned to the frontier Spaniards.[41]

Alonso reported that most prisoners were women and children, not adult warrior men, writing that "from May 1786 to May 1789, 610 Indian women and children but only 55 men were taken prisoners . . . They were sometimes exchanged for Hispanic captives, used as incentives in peace negotiations with the Apache, or forced to play a role in military strategy. They could also be allocated as a booty to reward presidial troops and settlers."[42]

Enslavement by Spaniards was not a new event to any of the Indians of northern Mexico. Rumors passed on told of Hernán Cortés marching into central Mexico in 1520–21 and subjugating the Mexihcahs, known today as the Aztecs. Indigenous peoples such as the Pima, Pápago, Seri, Ópata, Janos, Julimes, and others in northern Mexico also became the targets of European slave raiders. By 1539–40, when expeditions from Mexico City were exploring the northern reaches of Mexico, the Indians had developed a basic antagonism toward the Spaniards and "knew well enough the character of their would-be conquerors" because of word of mouth about the slavers who had been "raiding north from Culiacan for years . . . as far north as the Rio Sinaloa."[43] Two hundred years later, Jesuit Segesser, in a stunning denial of his own enslavement activities, noted that the Pimas were attacking the Seris and Apaches for the express purpose of "stealing their children. Slaves could be sold in exchange for trade goods and to gain favor with Spanish military leaders," he wrote.[44]

Slavery among the Chiricahuas and other northern Mexico tribes before the Spanish occupation was an accepted method of increasing the number of members. For example, one speculative scenario could occur during times of hardship. Perhaps a drought caused the desert's resources to diminish. In that case, competition for food and medicinal plants was intense and often led to conflict. The winners of the contest would take captives and incorporate them into their tribe; volunteers, impressed by the Chiricahuas' prowess and the probability of available food, often went along as well. In time, the captives would either remain or be traded back to their own tribes or to another tribe for whatever the Apaches wanted at the time. This process continued sporadically after the European occupation but was surpassed by the need, in the Apache mind, to protect from Spanish encroachment the land Ussen had given them. To the Chiricahuas, the frontier military establishment at Tubac was a significant offender for at least two reasons: captive Apaches were distributed to soldiers stationed there, and the Spaniards were invaders of the land the Indians had promised Ussen they would honor and protect.

Recruitment of Tubac's initial thirty-man presidial complement, including indigenous allies, was not difficult when returning Pimas, coming home in the mid-1700s after the Pima revolt, elected to enlist. True to the Spanish sense of superiority and dominion, segregated living arrangements prevailed in the new fort. Indians lived in thatch-roofed huts, ringed around the presidio's courtyard, unmarried officers shared adobe rooms facing the interior of the presidio's wall, and cavalrymen's shelters, initially made from poles and thatch—later adobe—lined a nearby road.

Four roads or paths led to and away from the presidio. One went southward toward the visita at Tumacácori, while a northward one went toward the indigenous groups and Spaniards living at San Xavier del Bac and Tucson.[45] An eastward path went toward the small mission at Sonoita, while another led westward and then southward toward the settlements of Altar and Tubutama in Sonora.[46]

"Around this post [Tubac] the first Spanish settlement of present Arizona grew," wrote Jones, possibly including farmers, ranchers, and military families having Apache slaves. "By 1757 the presidio and pueblo of Tubac counted 411 people . . . After 1759, under Captain Juan Bautista de Anza,[47] it was Pimeria Alta's principal settlement at the time."[48]

Along with military actions against Indians and protecting the nearby missions, the Tubac troopers had the additional responsibilities of escorting visiting civilian, religious, or military dignitaries, and riding beside supply trains, horse remount herds, or participating in excursions away from the fort. Oddly, Dobyns claims daily routines at the presidio could be uninteresting. "Tedium bred carelessness, and Apaches could

FIGURE 13 ∾ "Franciscan mission at Tumacácori." Sketch by Madeleine Smith, 2004.

FIGURE 14 ∾ "Franciscan missionary church at Tumacácori." Photo by Janet Eley, 2004.

often surprise," he wrote.[49] Yet, the continuing tension and busy activities at Tubac refute his assertion, especially with the possibility looming of an Apache attack at any time.

Without question, constant Apache surveillance of forts and settlements caused anxiety among the Europeans. Mark Santiago wrote, "They [the Apaches] scouted potential targets beforehand by detaching small groups . . . that gathered together in mountainous or rough terrain, from which they sallied forth in large numbers and overwhelmed local resistance."[50] His statement reveals one facet of the Apaches' effective attack strategy: a number of small groups from different locations joined forces at a predetermined time and place for a specific purpose and then quickly dispersed back to their various encampments, confusing the military authorities who were accustomed to their enemies all returning to one place. Consequently, military retaliation against the raiders was haphazard and disorganized, if it occurred at all. Since the Indians could not be identified as from one specific group, all Apaches in any area, regardless of their guilt or innocence, eventually were suspect, and action against the supposed offenders may not have been indicated at all, infuriating the wrongfully labeled Indians under attack and causing retaliation.

From sheltered sites in the hills around Tubac, Apaches observed the soldiers' comings and goings and formulated their raids accordingly. For example, the presidio's 1775 inventory of livestock included thirty-four mules. When the soldiers and some of those mules left the safety of the presidio to escort a pack train, Apaches had a choice. If they preferred to capture the animals, they could attack the train. They could instead raid the presidio, now weakened in the number of soldiers defending it, and run off the remaining livestock. Whatever their decision, the fort was just one of several targets.

Oral tradition told to Eve Ball in interviews with contemporary Mescalero, Chiricahua, and Lipan Apaches revealed that some astute farmers and ranchers on the colonial frontier kept their corrals filled with horses to satisfy the Apache raiders and thus kept kidnapping of people to a minimum. "They knew that if the Indians met with no resistance and got a good supply of mounts, they would not disturb the *hacienda* or its inhabitants. The Indians preferred to let cooperative Mexicans live in order to provide them with future supplies of horses.

If the Mexican ranchers were uncooperative . . . the Indians stole their women and children . . . The little girls were important because . . . the tribe did not increase rapidly."[51] The logical conclusion here is that the girls would become childbearing women, but they could also be traded back to Mexicans for commodities like sugar and bacon or swapped for Apache slaves other tribes or the Europeans held.

Besides anticipating Indian attacks and planning offensive actions, the Roman Catholic soldiers at Tubac were occasionally excited by the presence of a religious visitor to the presidio, usually stopping by to celebrate mass, baptize children and adults, and hear confessions. We may never know if killing Indians was viewed as a sin in the eyes of the church and, if so, what penance was assigned after the soldier's confession.

Beginning two years after the Pima revolt, Father Pauer periodically arrived at the presidio from Guévavi, eighteen miles south, to baptize the children of the fort's residents. For example, on New Year's Day 1754, he issued the sacrament to five children; returning six days later he baptized four more. In March, he baptized seven youngsters.

Baptism of indigenes was more than a sacrament—it was the ancient equivalent of identity theft. Never again would the child or adult carry a tribal name, nor would his descendants, unless something unexpected happened to reverse the process. Ancestral customs and heritage related to indigenous naming, especially the ceremonies, would be lost. Through the constant use of the new name, the individual would grow away from his tribe and closer to the Spaniards and Roman Catholicism. In time, connections to the indigenous lifeway would fade into the past, an irreparable tragedy.

The large volume of recorded baptisms all missionaries across northern Mexico performed is fascinating for its sheer numbers. I wish more information were available regarding the intent of the Indian parents and the steps of the process. It seems that no prior catechism classes for parents were necessary, nor was an understanding of the sacrament and its obligations conveyed adequately by priests who could not speak the native languages. A few words, some sprinkled water, and a documented entry in a ledger seems to have been the extent of it. In some frontier Indian societies, after the priests left, the tribes' shamans conducted reverse baptisms and purportedly undid the blessing. Although there is no evidence of this occurring among the Chiricahua Apaches, Perez

FIGURE 15 ∽ "Altar at Franciscan church—Tumacácori." Photo by Janet Eley, 2004.

noted that Perico, a member of northern Mexico's Acaxee tribe, "performed a series of rituals designed to undo, negate, co-opt, or reverse the spiritual work of the missionaries . . . Perico also changed the Spanish baptismal names of his followers back to indigenous names . . . [He] also made a point of divorcing Indian couples who had been married by the Catholic priests. Some were then married in a Native ceremony if they wanted to remain together."[52]

Another curious fragment of Spanish colonial history concerns the evolution of the name Tubac and is one example of the forced changes that occur when two diverse cultures clash. No doubt the Europeans had difficulty pronouncing Tchoowaka, the name of the Pima village, and so they probably changed the name to Tubaca. Dobyns traced Tchoowaka, back to a long-ago time in history when indigenous enemies raided the settlement and were killed by defending Pima/Sobaípuri warriors. As a measure of contempt, the tribe left the opponents' dead bodies out in the weather to decompose and then called the site Tchoowaka, which translates to "literally 'rotten.' By extension, the place name carries the connotation 'Place Where Some Enemies Rotted,'" Dobyns wrote.[53]

Kessell believes that the Jesuit Campos, Father Kino's close friend, first recorded the name Tubac in 1726. On his way to baptize twenty-five Indians at Tumacácori, he stopped to rest at Tubac, was asked to baptize a baby, and recorded the name of the rancheria as Tubac.[54] Administering other sacraments at Tubac occurred as well. In 1740, Alexandro Rapicani, SJ, performed a double marriage at Tubac for Francisco de Ortega and Gertrudis Barba and Luis Villela and Rosalía Durán; he recorded the event. Other records indicate that on May 23, 1741, Joseph de Torres Perea, SJ, then the resident priest at Guévavi, performed a wedding ceremony at Tumacácori, marrying the native Christian governor, Joseph Tutubusa and María Tupquice of San Xavier.[55] There is no evidence that medicine people reversed these Christian marriages.

Each time the missionaries appeared in the native villages, they distributed gifts and food to soften any resistance, then or in the future. Their philosophy licensed dishonesty. So, while at face value the welcome to perform religious activities seemed obvious, one must look twice at the reason for the Indians' friendly behavior. Along with bribery, speculation is that a belief among the indigenes was that the Spanish religious rites had some sort of magical power, for example, baptism would protect the natives from the diseases the newcomers brought. Whether this false idea was the product of the indigenous mind or was introduced by the Europeans has been lost to history. The fact remains that the priests infected the Indians by breathing on them as they sprinkled holy water on the Indians' heads.

A caveat is appropriate here. Readers should not compare the sacrament of baptism, as practiced today, with what the clergy performed on the frontier. The sheer number—hundreds of thousands—of adults and children baptized during the colonial era prohibited the catechumens being taught any of the principles of Roman Catholicism before receiving the sacrament.

As another explanation for the cordial receptions many priests experienced in the Indian villages, the age-old policy of divide and conquer had an immediate effect. The Spaniards convinced some tribes that an alliance with them would work in their favor against the more hostile tribes in the area, and many gullible Indians believed them. "The Spanish created much of the conflict that Indians sought to escape by aligning with them," wrote Perez. "Conversion to Christianity also required Indians to fight for the Spaniards . . . [R]efusal to confederate with the Spanish often resulted in becoming the object of Spanish attacks . . . Distinguishing oneself in military expeditions against Spanish enemies was one way for Christian Indians to gain recognition and prestige in the colonial system."[56]

Being accepted by the Europeans required a willingness on the part of the Indians to remain isolated from relatives and friends in their tribe through reducción. Once separated, however, in time many of the mission Indians accepted the Europeans' social control and shaped themselves to the newcomers' expectations. As time passed the acolytes, slaves, and mission Indians discarded their cultural identity and ancestral ways. For example, Tchoowaka, and all it had meant to so many Pimas, now allied with the Spaniards, receded into memory as did any physical or archeological evidence of the old village.

Clues to the type of housing in use before contact with the Europeans exist a few miles south of Tubac, where the remnants of a large native community have been discovered and unearthed. Dobyns labeled the ruins "adobe houses" and reported they were thick walled and located in clusters around a circular plaza.[57] Because the Tubac people's sustenance

FIGURE 16 ∾ "Mortuary at Tumacácori." Photo by author.

depended mainly on agriculture, however, not all Pimas lived as Dobyns reported. Many preferred grass-thatched pole homes erected in their fields, close to their crops and the sources of irrigation. The vast gardens they farmed produced maize, beans, squash, and cotton, all items able to be bartered with other Indians, the friendly Puebloans of New Mexico, the indigenous peoples of central Mexico, and the desert Pápago Indians who, in turn, traded dried cacti, fruits, mescal, chili peppers, acorns, dried venison, and mountain sheep tallow.[58]

By 1767, approximately fifteen years after the presidio of Tubac was founded, five hundred Europeans—mainly farmers, miners, ranchers, and their families—were living on and working the land that had once been the Tchoowakas' farming and hunting grounds. Anza had been successful in promoting a civilian settlement near or actually at the fort through word of mouth about the available free land, and the population continued to swell despite the well-known dangers from Apache assaults. "Pioneers at the . . . post were . . . spreading out with stock to graze these grassy uplands . . . Cattle ranching fitted the predilections of the frontiersmen . . . and they willingly rode herd through the thorny brush and over the steep slopes during round up time day after day," wrote Dobyns.[59] I could find no written documents describing the natives' reactions to the increasing census of newcomers into the area around Tubac or the loss of their homelands, but the continuing Indian attacks speak for themselves.

Some of the newcomers retained their European attitudes toward social classes and were acutely aware of their status vis-à-vis the Indians, the soldiers, and others in their immediate area. Although the indigenes far outnumbered the Europeans, the Spaniards were on the top rung of the ladder and as such were willing and eager to accept Indian slaves.[60] "Thus it was at the royal fort at Tubac," Dobyns wrote, adding,

> The incessant campaigns against the Apaches afforded ample opportunities for capturing likely young Apache girls and children to be reared as slaves or sold farther south. For Tubac the most important booty of Captain Anza's February-March campaign in 1766 was a group of fifteen Apache young women his detachment brought back to the post . . . [S]ome of them had recently become mothers. On a later campaign in the early 1770s, Captain Anza personally captured two young Apache children, a boy and a girl, who were baptized at Tumacacori Mission on February 13, 1774 . . . The boy was seven years old and the girl estimated to be eight to ten years. The priest who baptized them made a point of stating that Anza had "taken in just war" these two captives.[61]

To meet the religious needs of the growing number of settlers, particularly since the nearest missionary was located at Guévavi, eighteen miles away, Anza imported his wife's brother, a priest named Brother Joseph Manuel Díaz de Carpio, to serve as presidial chaplain at Tubac. Carpio recorded two baptisms in February 1760 and one each in September and October; the latter two new Christians were from the mission at Tumacácori. The inference here is that baptisms occurred either at Tubac or Tumacácori whenever a priest was in the area, regardless of where the new Christians lived.

Dobyns also documented the birth rate at Tubac for certain years, although he was not always precise on the infant's ethnicity. For example, beginning in November 1752 two children were born to wives of soldiers. The next year nine births were recorded. In 1754, two babies were born, the next year, four. In 1756, there were three, followed in 1757 by two. Six women bore children in 1758, and three births occurred in 1759.[62] Dobyns noted that "some of the children born to Tubac mothers were born out of wedlock, often in other settlements."[63] Paternity did not seem important enough to be noted. Who were the fathers? Indians or soldiers? Civilians or priests?

Opposite of the birth rate was the number of deaths. Other than from warfare, deaths at Tubac were mainly the result of recurrent epidemics that struck periodically. Starting in 1758 an unknown illness, possibly a viral infection of some sort, affected the indigenous populations at Guévavi, Tumacácori, and Sonoita; somehow it skipped Tubac. Thirty-six Indians died, twenty-one of whom were buried inside the fledgling church at Tumacácori. Dobyns attributes the lack of fatalities at Tubac to the fact that the illness was more deadly to the Indians than to the Spaniards or to mixed bloods living at the fort, all of whom probably had some degree of immunity. In February 1766 all Sonora suffered heavy mortality from an ailment, possibly typhus, that caused high fever, delirium, vomiting, and bleeding. Measles and yellow fever were next, infecting the mission at Santa María Magdalena in January 1770 and spreading to San Ignacio and Guévavi in February and March. Tubac experienced the illness, but no one perished.[64]

The mission Indians clearly faced a dilemma. If they remained under Spanish authority they were vulnerable to the contagious diseases that were destroying their population. Attacks by marauding tribes on the missions also killed some indigenes, accidentally or deliberately, and so they risked death in that way. Yet if these neophytes left the mission to rejoin their still-free companions, they were subjected to intense, deadly warfare from the presidial soldiers stationed all across the frontier. Possible retaliation at home against any returnees for their actions in leaving the camp and taking up residence with the Europeans was also possible. If a decision became necessary, many indigenes opted to remain in the missions as their best choice and face death from diseases rather than the fury of Spanish guns or tribal retaliation.

Word of the deteriorating situation on the far reaches of New Spain

FIGURE 17 ∞ "Mortuary chapel at Tumacácori." Photo by Janet Eley, 2004.

FIGURE 18 ∞ "Cemetery at Tumacácori." Photo by author.

had earlier come to the attention of Carlos III who, in 1767, sent two emissaries, the visitor general, José de Gálvez, and the Marqués de Rubí, a member of Gálvez's staff, to assess the Indian problems. Even though the Apaches had been receiving most of the blame for the frontier depredations, they were not solely responsible for the destruction. Other marauding bands raided and robbed on a regular basis. Some clever warriors from other tribes disguised their true identity by wearing Apache war caps, but this is not to dismiss the Apaches' predominant role in the raids.[65]

At the conclusion of his tour, Gálvez recommended a large-scale military operation including punitive expeditions against all the belligerent Indians, "trade alliances, and balance of power tactics."[66]

In northern Sonora, Rubí saw firsthand the effects of the Apache raids. Spanish settlers had been killed; burned, abandoned ranches proliferated across the countryside; livestock had been stolen; and crop fields destroyed. Rubí concluded that the Apaches had to be removed from the area through increased force until no respite or refuge was available to them. Additionally, he suggested that a wholesale realignment of the existing presidios to contain the situation would be effective against the Apaches. Furthermore, "to eliminate this menace, he [Rubí] advocated a systematic extermination of the Apaches, and the forwarding of captive families south to be distributed in the interior of Mexico," noted Joseph Park.[67] In other words, any Indians who fought to preserve their homelands and their way of life and were captured were to be deported and enslaved elsewhere.

Rubí's suggestions were eventually embodied in the New Regulations of 1772. Sidney B. Brinckerhoff and Odie B. Faulk quoted the 1772 Reglamento regarding prisoners of war.

> They shall be sent to the vicinity of Mexico City where [the] viceroy may dispose of them as seems convenient . . . In no case shall the Indians arrested be sent into servitude as has illegally been done in the past; instead they will be treated and assisted as prescribed for prisoners of war . . . [W]omen and children are to be treated with gentleness, restoring them to their parents and families in order that they recognize that it is . . . the administration of justice that motivates our laws.[68]

So the men were not to be immediately enslaved but sent to Mexico City, where the viceroy could distribute them as slaves, if that was his wish; the women and children were to be returned to their parents and families. Since no further instructions regarding the method this "restoration" would take were offered, however, it would be up to the military officers to decide their destiny.

Significantly, the official document also stated that if the Apaches chose to "subject themselves to the king's domination," that is, surrender, or "offered strict guarantees" that they would be peaceful, the hostilities against them would cease.[69] In other words, the choices for the Apaches were surrender, enslavement, death, or, for the women and children, a return to their families.

A well-known officer, Hugo O'Conor, commandant inspector of all the presidios on the frontier, was scheduled to review Tubac after Rubí's recommendation to realign the presidios so as to more effectively control the frontier. O'Conor had the final decision whether Tubac's presidio and its military personnel would be removed to Tucson. For ten intensive days, he and his staff reviewed the small fortress and then he issued a scathing report.

> The height of this troop is substandard, as are its state of health, fitness, and physical strength. Although skilled in horsemanship, they lack the first rudiments of military discipline and standard operational procedure, confining themselves to no more than guarding the barracks . . . Even though there may be positive reports that some of the enemy have entered the province, this troop does not bestir itself to pursue them.[70]

As if that were not bad enough, O'Conor had this to say about Tubac's residents.

> The civilian population congregated at this presidio is composed of forty-one families of gente de razon [non-Indians], two of Opata Indians, one of Piros (a tribe of the middle Rio Grande in New Mexico), and one of Apaches. Yet all are so wretched that one cannot count on their permanence in this presidio once

the troop is transferred to its new station at Tucson. It is to be expected that they will follow . . .[71]

In 1776 the presidio was relocated. Unhappy villagers that year, numbering 150 persons, were naturally fearful and worried about the lack of protection and danger from raiding Indians. Earlier in the year there had been a devastating Apache assault at Tumacácori during which the church had been damaged as the marauding Indians carried off everything they could find. Tubac's residents complained loudly to local officials about the move, insisting that they were constantly at risk, but it seemed at the time that they were correct; no one listened or cared.

Raiding Apaches, always opportunists, next stole the settlement's entire herd of horses. One month later the same Apaches taunted Tubac's villagers by pasturing their own herd, some of which had previously belonged to local ranchers, in a nearby field and then loading up with stolen maize before leaving. Friar Ximeno wrote about what the residents, now a mix of Spaniards, Mexicans, and Indians, could expect from him whenever the Apaches appeared: "The only help the priests can give the [people] is to hide with them from the same arrows."[72]

Despite appearances to the contrary, the colonists' protests had not been totally ignored; a small detachment of twelve to fourteen soldiers returned to the area and guarded not only Tubac but also the missions at Tumacácori and Calabazas as well. This meant nothing to the Apaches and in the early autumn of 1778, they attacked Tubac again and stole five horses from the restored herd. In October they returned for the cattle, running off the small number of livestock the villagers had managed to accumulate. Undoubtedly fearful and frustrated, Tubac's residents turned to the Franciscans at Tumacácori for comfort as they had done so many times in the past. Still, nothing seemed to stem the relentless Indian attacks, and by 1783 the survivors gave up. Tubac was totally abandoned but Tumacácori's mission remained, separated from its neighboring village for the first time in its long history.

Tumacácori's name translates to "flat and rock" or "place of the flat rock," a reference to a geological formation on the base of a nearby mountain.[73] When Jesuit Kino and Father Visitor Juan María Salvatierra, SJ, first visited Tumacácori in January 1691, Father Kino noted the people were docile, industrious, affable, and lived in a beautiful fertile and pleasant

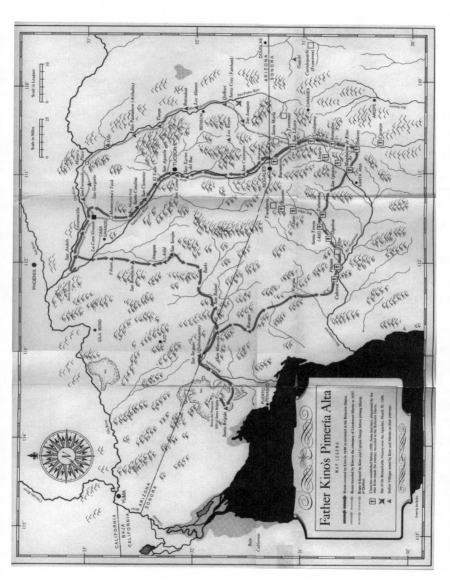

MAP 3 ❦ "Father Kino's Pimería Alta." From Fay Jackson Smith, John L. Kessell, and Francis J. Fox, SJ, *Father Kino in Arizona* (Phoenix: Arizona Historical Foundation, 1966). Reprinted with permission of Arizona Historical Foundation.

valley with mild winters. The indigenes gave him the impression they would like to have a Jesuit living among them, but a description of how that wish was expressed to a European is not available.[74] After a long ten to eleven years, the cabecera of Guévavi was established with San Cayetano de Tumacácori as one of its visitas. In the interim, Father Kino's description of the Indians as "industrious" underwent a change Father Segesser noted when he wrote that "without supervision the Pimas would not grow European crops or tend their trees."[75] The contrasting descriptions were an example of contradictions that occurred frequently when individual missionaries evaluated the Indians. Each priest used his own subjective evaluation criteria, as no objective standards existed to guide the clergy in their assessments, a fact that became particularly troublesome when the revolving-door priests changed assignments. If the Indians had grown accustomed to shaping themselves to meet the expectations of their familiar resident priest, they had to stop short and change their ways to meet the wishes of the newly arrived clergyman, not an easy effort for a preliterate people, probably frightened and insecure.

Another change would also take place soon after the switch in administration. The new priest's selection of an indigenous liaison was important for him to create a smooth transition and continuity, but his choice might be different in personality and attitude from the former entrenched go-between. The intermediary's ego could also portend a difficult adjustment, especially if the tribal members disliked the selected headman, who was now in a position to repay a few debts. Familiar, daily work schedules previously assigned to specific persons could switch overnight, disrupting a routine that had become customary and comfortable but now required another trial-and-error period. The new priest's styles of punishment might also deviate from what the people were accustomed to. Whereas one thought a minor infraction necessitated shaving the offender's hair, for example, the next clergyman's preference would be the whip for the same indiscretion.

Tumacácori suffered from revolving-door priests as much as the other missions did. Nothing could be done to alter the situation, however, as the causes for the substitutions were often beyond everyone's control and mostly related to medical situations or deaths from warfare, which seemed unending. After the Pima revolt of 1751, for example, Tumacácori was moved across the water to be closer to the protection offered by Tubac. Tumacácori then became an "artificial congregation," reported Kessell, noting that in 1753 Tubac's presidial soldiers rounded up the Pimas and Pápagos who had returned to their village and then resettled them at Tumacácori.[76] At this time, a new patron saint was identified as San José and the village renamed San José de Tumacácori.

Kessell's reference to an "artificial congregation" was not clear but could be interpreted to mean that Tubac's homecoming natives did not voluntarily join the community at Tumacácori. Expanding Kessell's theory, I believe that forcing the returnees to relocate was deliberate and planned, allowed the soldiers and their families to preempt the good land at Tubac for their own uses, and obviously was a continued use of reducción/congregación insofar as opening the land for Spanish settlement. Here again, nothing could be done on behalf of the natives who might have wanted to remain at Tchoowaka.

In the mid- to late 1700s, there was substantial Indian activity on the frontier, some of it hostile, some peaceful. Along with Tubac's people coming home at the end of the Pima revolt in 1751, Father Pauer, stationed at Guévavi, started to supervise erecting a church at Tumacácori in 1757.[77] This was a needed endeavor for, with the continuing influx of indigenes, "by 1760 it [Tumacácori] had become the [Jesuit] mission's largest and most active village."[78] Statistics dated 1761 reveal seventy-two families at Tumacácori, with only thirty-one at Guévavi, thirty-six at the visita of Calabazas, and thirty-four at the visita of Sonoita.[79] European diseases, always killers, continued to strike with as much vehemence as did the Apaches, who constantly raided ranches, farms, missions, mines, and anything else that appealed to them. Warfare on the colonial frontier had reached unprecedented levels and finally became cause for serious worry among Spanish authorities, local and in Mexico City. Something had to be done. One solution, the authorities reasoned, was to increase the number of mission residents, thus improving protection and possibly intimidating attackers.

A number of Sobaípuri villages, east of the San Pedro River in what is now far southeastern Arizona, had usually served as buffers against Apache assaults farther west. These Pima cousins were not under the control of any missions in the mid-1700s. Not a timid people, they had occasionally aligned themselves with the Spaniards, but now, with diseases and Apache warfare destroying the missions, the Sobaípuris became

FIGURE 19 ∞ "Recreated ramada where early religious services were held at
Tumacácori mission." Photo by author, October 1998.

very important to the Spaniards. The governor and captain general of
Sonora, José Tienda de Cuervo, signed an order requiring Sobaípuris to
be moved into missions at Suamca and Sonoita, supporting the notion
that the missions would be better able to defend themselves with more
residents. The Sobaípuris, 250 in all, were quickly and forcibly moved
from their rancherias and relocated in missions. The theory was seriously
flawed, however. With the eastern reaches of the valley now empty and
vulnerable because the Sobaípuri fighters had been forcibly transferred,
all hell broke loose. Apaches attacked at will, leaving almost nothing in
their wake. "The Apaches kept coming," wrote Kessell, in an understate-
ment about Apache activities during 1763. "Along the valley from Soamca
through Guevavi to San Xavier del Bac, no one was safe working in the
fields or riding herd. On moonlit nights especially, vaqueros drove their
stock into corrals. Mission Indians and settlers alike were terrorized."[80]

Father Ximeno wanted to abandon Guévavi that year, 1763, because
there was next to nothing left; it had been literally destroyed by disease
and continuing Apache raids. The father visitor, Manuel Aguirre, SJ, had
another suggestion, though it was ultimately ignored: divide Guévavi in

two with Tumacácori as a cabecera and Calabazas as its visita. Sonoita would remain under Guévavi's jurisdiction.[81]

Two years earlier, Sonoita's population had surpassed that of Guévavi and Tumacácori, an event attributable to the infusion of the San Pedro valley Sobapaípuris to Sonoita and a deadly epidemic that reduced the populations of the two other missions. By December 1766, the village of Guévavi had shrunk to fifty people, and Calabazas was nearly annihilated. Struggling against the odds, both sites hung on for a time, particularly Calabazas; its days as a visita ended in 1786.[82]

It was left to the Franciscans to apply the Jesuit father visitor's suggestion of years earlier. When fifteen Franciscans—by 1772 nine more were in the Sonoran missions[83]—entered the Santa Cruz valley in 1768, Father Gil de Bernabé was initially stationed at Guévavi.[84] Immediately recognizing the mission's desperate straits, he wanted to move the religious headquarters to Tumacácori, but it took three years to change the former visita into a cabecera.

Under the guidance of Francisco Zúñiga, OFM, who replaced Father Gil de Bernabé, a daily routine structured the Indians' behavior at Tumacácori. Every day at sunrise bells rang announcing mass. Selected native headmen awakened the people and shepherded them to the church before directing them to their workplaces. In the evening, the labor-weary Indians were required to attend mass before going to their homes. On Sundays everyone had to appear at the church, well washed, clean clothed, with combed hair for the mass. Penance and holy communion were part of the process. During holy seasons, selected neophytes were required to participate in processions that honored saints and other religious icons.

The two Franciscans in charge of Tumacácori in 1772—Ximeno and Gaspar de Clemente—renovated certain sections of the mission. For example, unhappy with the Indians' traditional housing—mud and brush huts with dirt floors—they instructed their neophytes to tear down the huts and rebuild the living quarters out of adobe. Next, they turned their attention to the existing Jesuit church and refurbished it. After that was completed, up went an adobe wall, supposedly to keep out Apache raiders who were bolder than ever in their assaults. Nothing seemed to stop them as they "stole mission livestock, burned buildings, broke statues, and mocked the priests," wrote Christopher Vecsey.[85]

Frustrated, in March 1773 Father Ximeno wrote a letter to colleagues at the Franciscan college in Querétero, Mexico.

> As long as the government fails to provide more prompt, active, and efficacious measures to contain the Apaches, not only will the missions not be advanced, but neither will it be possible to promote new conversions and just expansion of His Majesty's dominions. Even what is already conquered will be lost . . . All that will be said is . . . over there once stood a mission called Tumacacori . . . but [it was] destroyed by Apaches.[86]

That summer Father Ximeno left Tumacácori, reassigned to the mission at Pitic. Father Clemente remained and was joined by Joseph Matías Moreno, OFM.[87] By 1774, Guévavi and Sonita had been abandoned, destroyed physically and emotionally by unrelenting assaults from human and medical causes. The visita of Calabazas was on its way to becoming a stock ranch at the end of the 1780s. Only Tumacácori remained religiously vital, now peopled with refugees from the other three.

Fathers Clemente and Moreno remained at Tumacácori until 1774, baptizing twenty-nine Pimas, Pápagos, settlers from Tubac, Indian slaves known as Níxoras, whom Indians traded to Indians, and a few Apache children. Replacing the friars were Pedro Antonio Arriquibar, OFM, and Tomás Eixarch, OFM. A year later, Tumacácori's census showed ninety-one Pimas and Pápagos, and twenty-six settlers. The livestock count stood at about one hundred cattle, twelve mares and twelve horses, and a thousand sheep.[88]

By 1780, Fathers Arriquibar and Eixarch were reassigned, and Baltazar Carillo, OFM, assumed the administration of Tumacácori. A terrible smallpox epidemic hit in 1781, killing 10 percent of the Indians within five weeks; twenty-two others died of various causes during the next six years. Not mentioned was syphilis, but it was apparently spreading throughout the missions near the end of the decade as "an unsavory bunch of syphilitic boys . . . hung around Saric."[89]

Sexually transmitted diseases were likely unknown in most Indian villages before contact with the Europeans. It should be remembered, however, that trade routes to and from central Mexico existed before the Spaniards arrived on the northern frontier, so it is possible that these ailments had been introduced there, but were not widespread. Curiosity leads me to wonder if any of the missionaries were guilty of spreading syphilis. Several authors have addressed aspects of this issue. For example, Frank de la Teja and Ross Frank wrote that

> the violation of celibacy was commonplace in the Iberian world and was not considered to be particularly grievous unless it occurred as a result of solicitation in the confessional. As

FIGURE 20 ∞ "Colegio de Propaganda Fide, Querétaro." From Zephyrin Englehardt, OFM, *Franciscans in Arizona* (Harbor Springs, MI: Holy Child Indian School, 1899).

other scholars have pointed out, Catholic clergymen were in an anomalous position in a world where masculinity was heavily tied to sexual activity. This helps to explain why priestly liaisons were tolerated as long as they were relatively discreet.[90]

It is not much of a leap to speculate that the missionaries and the soldiers may have introduced syphilis to native women or have been infected through intercourse with Spanish, Mexican, or Indian women and would, in turn, have passed on the affliction themselves.

In 1786 only one hundred indigenes remained at Tumacácori, but the next year an eighty-person Pima Indian military company reoccupied Tubac to fight the increasing Apache presence. Apaches seemed to be everywhere, uncontrollable, raiding and taunting, setting fires, screaming, killing livestock, and taking advantage of every opportunity. Under the Instructions of 1786, intensified military campaigns against the Apaches were quickly instituted, and the Chiricahuas realized that this time the Spaniards were more serious than ever. There was a choice now, however: the Indians could voluntarily surrender at the new "peace establishments" and avoid warfare. Though some did, others did not and continued raiding, but during the near future, Apache attacks decreased, and an intermittent sigh of relief blew across the colonial frontier as more and more pragmatic Chiricahuas checked into the peace establishments.

Beginning July 10, 1794, Narciso Gutiérrez, OFM, joined Father Carillo at Tumacácori. A little more than one year later Father Carillo died and was buried in front of the church's main altar. During the next five years, Father Gutiérrez would be assisted by five missionaries, none of whom was happy or stayed for long. The problem this time was Father Gutiérrez himself, a young man with a difficult personality who was ultimately, over his strong objections, removed from his post at Tumacácori and transferred to Tubutama in 1797.[91] Unhappy and angry while at Tubutama, Father Gutiérrez developed a plan to return to Tumacácori. He met with and convinced some of his former charges to appeal to the father president, Francisco Iturralde, OFM, to have him resume his work at Tumacácori. Father Iturralde saw through the scheme and refused, although Gutiérrez's change of heart and improved personality restored him, two years later, to his position at Tumacácori.

In 1796, Mariano Bordoy, OFM, and Ramón López, OFM, were stationed at Tumacácori and conducted a census that same year. They recorded 103 individuals, including 3 listed as "Spanish." Whiting speculated that 1 may have been a priest's housekeeper, and 2—a boy of eleven and a girl of three—orphans. The largest group of residents were Pápagos, age thirty and older; a third were Pimas; 1 person was identified as Yuma; and 1 Apache boy captured in a raid. He was subsequently baptized and named Manuel María Arcilla and was listed as living at Tumacácori even though he was being "educated in Tucson." The true meaning of that phrase may never be known. Captive children and others were distributed to families, near and far, who promised to educate them and raise them in the Roman Catholic faith. In reality many became slaves in their owners' households, and this may have been Manuel's fate.

Also listed among Tumacácori's residents in 1796 were ten Juans, ten Josés, and seventeen Marías, widowers and widows, single men, girls of all ages, boys of all ages, married couples, and people identified only as from the surrounding area. Thirty-five Pimas, twenty-eight Pápagos, twelve Yaquis, and one Ópata were Christians. The largest percentage of all residents were between the ages of twenty and twenty-nine, the two eldest were between seventy and seventy-nine years old.

Apache raids on Tumacácori and other missions decreased dramatically at the end of the eighteenth century as large groups of Chiricahuas learned they could be removed from their homelands and enslaved, either in Mexico City's environs or in far-off Cuba. Many appeared unexpectedly at the newly named peace establishments, some of which were formerly missions only.

One of the peace establishments in particular, the Janos, Mexico, facility, became quickly overcrowded with Apaches seeking refuge from the all-out military effort against them and the consequences of capture, if they survived. Janos was a centrally located site in Sonora's neighboring state, Chihuahua, notable for its presidio, mission, and the Apache experience.[92] The earliest settlement of Janos included Franciscan missionaries in approximately 1580; Indians killed them shortly thereafter. One hundred years later Apache raiders destroyed the original mission, still standing unoccupied. Nothing was rebuilt until six years later when a military outpost was garrisoned there, but no peace was attainable between the Spaniards and local tribes, particularly the Janos and Jocomes indigenes until 1704; no reference to Apaches was noted.[93] By the 1750s, records of encounters with Apaches became more detailed and showed Chiricahua women coming to the Janos presidio and mission asking for food and other supplies. For example, in April 1757, despite ongoing hostilities, a lone, old Apache woman carrying a black wooden cross walked up to the presidio and asked for peace. The officials gave her corn, tobacco, and other gifts to take back to her encampment where she likely distributed the items according to custom. Six days later three Apache men strode out of the desert toward the presidio, each carrying a similar cross, each asking for gifts. On June 16, five Apaches, including the wife of a headman, did the same.

In August 1757 Apaches stole horses; in September they ran off a herd of steers from Janos. On October 10, four Apache women arrived at the fort and told the officials that their chief wanted to trade Spanish captives for cows, horses, and clothing. Immediately afterward a patrol left the presidio to find the captives and hunt Apaches but was unsuccessful. On October 25, a war party struck a large hacienda, and even though twenty soldiers tracked them, the Apaches successfully disappeared.[94]

In a 1760 military campaign, Apache chief Chafalote was killed; his sons were killed two years later. In 1771 military companies from Janos and San Buenaventura fought Apaches for six days at Sierra de la Boca. One year later a group of about two hundred attacked the Janos presidio. Later that year Apache leaders petitioned for peace at Janos and San Buenaventura; the effort failed. From 1774 through 1777, attacks and battles occurred many times with fatalities on both sides. Violence and death continued until Apache leaders El Zurdo, Pachatijú, and Natanijú attempted to make peace with Narciso de Tapia and other Janos officials in 1777, but their offer was refused. El Zurdo left the Janos area in 1787 for points unknown, possibly Cuba. One year later Pachatijú was captured and removed from Janos, likely sent to Cuba. That same year a Chiricahua chief, El Compá, aligned himself and his followers with the Spaniards; they lived at Janos. The next few years saw a rise in the number of peaceful contacts and activities. Chief Squielnoctero and his family sought refuge at Janos in 1789. In 1790 a leader named Ojos Colorados (probably Mangas Coloradas) made peace, but there is no mention in these documents of his living at Janos. In 1792 Manta

FIGURE 21 ❧ "Mission church at Janos." Photo by Perrie Barnes, 2003.

FIGURE 22 ∞ "Baptismal font in mission church at Janos." Photo by Perrie
  Barnes, 2003.

Negra the Elder lived at Janos for nine months.[95] For years afterward, the
relationship between the Janos military and Apaches from surrounding
encampments was one of love-hate, as it had been in the earlier years
of the century, and the terrible Apache raids continued, interrupted by
occasional bursts of short peace.

   In the late 1790s, ten to sixteen Chiricahua Apache settlements, all
headed by different chiefs, dotted the countryside around Janos, receiving food and other supplies until the crops they planted grew to maturity.
The following year many Apaches, unhappy with being restrained, fled
the mission and returned to their encampments; others remained. On
May 1, 1799, a Janos rancheria led by Nibora (also known as Vívora) contained thirty-two men and fifty-two women and children living in peace.
His colleague Vit-sago's rancheria held thirty-six men and forty-eight
women and children. Tasquenelte's and Gandules's rancheria census
was not available. By December 31, 1799, the population had increased
dramatically from four villages to sixteen, led by Yoza, Lucas, Vívora,
Marcos, Tecolero, El Compá, Tesquenelte, Toribio, Autingli, Tagarlan,
Juan Diego, Setado, Ygnacio, Seledio, Guero, and Perico.[96]

Around that time, during the swirl of activity related to trading, raiding, and settling in at the peace establishment, the military's central command was also directed to cut costs at Janos and decrease the number of Apaches receiving rations. Military officials responded by urging the Apaches to return to their local units. Confused, most Chiricahuas complied and headed for their old, traditional campsites. When the practice of releasing peaceful Apaches had been in effect for about one year, nearly 70 percent of the former mission residents were back home and resuming their familiar lifeways, including raiding and fighting.

In 1794 the Apaches counted at Janos had numbered 850. In the late months of 1796 only 200 remained, and a year after that the number fell to 130. More than 500 Apaches had returned to their old ways within a few years just at the peace establishment of Janos alone.

What of those Apaches taken captive during the military campaigns conducted earlier around Janos and other peace establishments? Were the prisoners deported? Sold as slaves? One unusual answer appears: Cuba.

While the Reglamento of 1772 authorized the deportation of captured warriors and their families to Mexico City, some Spanish officers began to consider sending the Apaches to Cuba. In 1783 the crown approved an order calling for the deportation of Chiricahua prisoners of war, including those already incarcerated in Mexico City, to a place from which they could not return, Cuba. Once on the island, the Apaches were to be distributed among Cuban families who would agree to convert and educate the Indians in the doctrines of the church. Most of the women and children were placed in homes, but the men represented a special problem. If they could not be allocated, they were required to work fortifying the docks. How the distribution of the men, women, and children would be decided once they arrived remains a mystery. No Cuban records are available.

In January 1783 a contingent of 145 Apaches of both sexes left the state of Chihuahua, marching under guard to Mexico City, where the viceroy was empowered to decide their fate. Fifty-six managed to escape, 9 were killed in the attempt, and 47 made good the effort. Of these, 14 were women and 2 were infants. The Europeans learned that neither age nor health status was a determinant of the will to be free. Archer reported that "even the very young Indians of ten to twelve years could escape and eventually find their way back to the north, posing a serious threat to the Spanish because of the knowledge they had picked up."[97] That is, if they survived; many died en route.

Moorhead stated that the officers were required to report problems, including illnesses and deaths, and were to record which of the dying Apaches had been "baptized and whether or not they were buried in consecrated ground, but seldom the nature of their illness." For example, "Of the 108 Apaches [on the way to Mexico City] in 1788, only seventy-three arrived . . . an undecipherable number of Apache girls was left . . . with a captain [along the route] who requested them."[98]

Some of the fugitives of all ages avoided recapture and found their way back to their encampments, where they were more furious than ever at the Spanish occupiers. Certain of these became new leaders of the increasingly ferocious Apache raids and assaults. When word of the large number of escapees reached Spain, in July 1788 the crown responded by issuing a royal decree, "requiring the viceroy to insure that prisoners arriving in Mexico City in the future could never return to their homeland and renew their depredations."[99] Archer explained the resultant policy, writing that "by 1789, deportation of the [captured] Chiricahuas to Havana, Cuba, was a generally accepted activity."[100] In the late 1790s the captain general of Cuba, the Marqués de Someruelos, tried to stop the deportation, claiming that the arrived Apaches caused numerous inconveniences and disruptions in Cuba.[101] It seems that the long land and sea journeys had reinforced the people's spirit rather than breaking it.

Salvation Through Slavery

๙2 DEATH, DEPORTATION, OR CONFINEMENT: THESE AND NO OTHER choices faced the Chiricahua Apaches during the intensive military campaigns against them in the late 1700s. The consequences of any of the three, authorized by the Instructions of 1786, were disastrous. The fates of the resisters and their families were to be killed, jailed, consigned indefinitely to workhouses, transferred to Cuba, or enslaved. Volunteers who surrendered and moved into the peace establishments entered a life of unending hard work and possible death from contagious diseases or Apache raids; no one was spared.

By October 1, 1787, Col. Jacobo Ugarte y Loyola reported that "his forces had killed 294 . . . captured another 305, liberated 15 of their own captives and induced several bands" to surrender. Seventeen of the warriors from this battle were dispatched in chains to Guadalajara for disposition. The women's fate is unclear, but an unknown number of children were transferred to Real de los Álamos to be sold to private owners "with the expectation that accommodating citizens would rear, dress, educate, and Christianize them."[1] The children supposedly would realize salvation through slavery but only if their purchasers were moral and upstanding citizens. If not, the promises of Christianity would be empty.

As time went on, more and more Apaches were shipped to Cuba. In 1788 Ugarte captured 125 Apaches, and 55 others surrendered voluntarily; these eventually marched to Mexico City and the port of Veracruz for placement. Moorhead writes that a group of just one hundred Apaches who had been captured in Sonora were dispatched . . . in January of 1789 with a train of forty-eight mules. Each mule probably carried two or more prisoners, for forty-six of them were infants and children under the age of six. The trip, amounting to something over 1,500 miles, took seventy-five days. An officer and seventeen troopers . . . escorted the train.[2]

Agreeing that "most captives were women and children," Elizabeth A. H. John then asks,

> What must have been the impact of those losses upon the small Apache family camps? How many Apache families had to seize and adopt women and children of other peoples to replace their own lost women and children? Of the Apaches sold south, how many lived to be assimilated into the populations of the mining provinces? . . . The questions stand unanswerable but they suggest tremendous ferment among all peoples affected and a much wider circle of involvement than was immediately obvious.[3]

Thomas Hall also writes about the situation, but from the point of view of the military.

> It seemed that enslavement . . . was the main answer to the problem of soldier recruiting—without the hope of Indian slaves to sell, an adequate soldiery on the frontier would have been even more difficult to maintain than it was . . . The old Spanish customs of requiring soldiers to supply their own equipment combined with insufficient funding of military operations, encouraged the taking and selling of captives.[4]

Charles Gibson notes the historical basis for enslavement. "In general, the first Spanish contacts with the natives of America followed the precedent of European contact with the natives of the Africa, and the practicality and legitimacy of enslavement were everywhere assumed."[5] And why not? Slave hunting and selling could make someone a good living. "Throughout the seventeenth century, Spanish residents paid fifty to one hundred pesos for licenses to go out into the wilds and enslave groups of Indians on the pretext of bringing them into Hispanic society for the purpose of civilizing and Christianizing them."[6] In other words, salvation through slavery.

Spain's initial reaction to slaveholding in the New World, back in the sixteenth century, was hypocritical. As a reigning Catholic monarch in the 1500s, Queen Isabella condemned the practice and claimed to take seriously the moral obligation to Christianize the native populations but contradicted herself by demanding at times a share in the trade of Indian captives as slaves.[7] Simultaneously, she also recognized and approved the need to discipline captured, resistant indigenes. As a result of experience in administering and organizing captives, two colonial institutions arose in central Mexico after Cortés. Writing about one, the encomienda, Cutter and Engstrand state that

> In theory [the encomienda] was a means whereby native people under the guidance of trustworthy Spanish citizens were to be instructed in the way of becoming not only good vassals of the crown but also Christian citizens. In practice . . . it became an opportunity to become wealthy at the expense of the labor of the Indians.[8]

Trustworthy Spaniards, known as encomenderos, were agents of the empire who held the right to tributes produced by coerced native labor. "The object of encomienda was to Christianize pagan peoples through the ministrations of the *encomenderos* and to civilize them by encouraging orderly habits of industry," wrote Gibson. "To the *encomenderos* the encouragement . . . meant only that permission was given for forced labor."[9] Here again was the expectation of salvation, but the reality was often quite different, especially in terms of the tributes the slaves were expected to pay the encomenderos. The captured Indians, terrified of reprisals if they refused the Spaniards' requests, "gave everything they had," quoted Gibson.

> As the tributes, however, were so continuous that they barely paid one when they were obliged to pay another, they sold their children and their lands to money lenders in order to meet their

obligations; and when they were unable to do so, many died because of it, some under torture and some in cruel prisons for the Spaniards treated them brutally and considered them less than beasts.[10]

If encomienda was individual in nature, repartimiento, the second institution, was collective. Weber described it euphemistically as a "time honored institution by which Spanish officials distributed native men to work on a rotating basis at tasks deemed to be for the public good."[11] In other words, repartimiento dispersed involuntary Indian workers to Spanish employers such as ranchers, farmers, miners, or other colonists in need of physical labor in their efforts to ostensibly improve the "public good," whatever that was. Questions arise. Who controlled the pool of Indians workers to be distributed? What were the criteria for selection? Who apportioned them to which employers using what standards? What happened to them if they escaped and were recaptured?

During a lecture in 2001, Polzer did not discuss that aspect of life in central Mexico but was quite candid in defining repartimiento as "essentially slavery."[12] Polzer's words express the truth, as participation was compulsory, but the natives were supposed to receive wages, and regulations theoretically controlled the length of their servitude and the type of labor they were expected to do. Whether these provisions were actually met is arguable.

Other conditions of repartimiento called for a mandatory thirty-days' rest between assignments and stipulated that the workers were not to be taken out before sunrise nor brought back after sunset and were to have an hour's rest at noon. Half a gold peso per year was their reward. One incredible fact of life for these workers was being branded. Simpson wrote that they were "sent off to the mines chained together . . . duly branded with the iron of his Majesty, which is to be kept in the strong-box of the cabildo [town council]."[13]

Robert Miller and William Orr address branding of slaves and prisoners on the colonial frontier, stating that "both men and women are branded on their backs with a hot iron, each slave-holding household using its own mark. Every slave they buy must submit to the agony of branding so that, if they flee and are captured again, their masters can immediately be identified."[14] Cuello adds, "Encomienda Indians were branded, often several times by a succession of claimants to their persons. Inevitably, Spaniards wound up killing each other over their Indians."[15]

This unspeakable atrocity occurred five hundred years ago on a frontier nearly ten thousand miles from the seat of power in Madrid at a moment in history when standards reflected the cruel climate of the times and included many "acceptable" methods of brutality toward indigenes. Still, when Carlos I heard a rumor that the conquistadors and other settlers in the New World were disobeying his directives regarding the decent treatment of the Indians, he asserted his authority through legal means.

The New Laws, passed in 1542–43, were one of his attempts to direct the events in New Spain by means of humanitarian measures and ensure the supreme power of the crown in the New World. Of the fifty-four articles in the laws, twenty-three concerned the status and treatment of the Indians. For example, Article 26 states that

> for no reason of war or any other, even though it be by reason of rebellion or purchase, may any Indian be made a slave, and we wish them to be treated as our vassals of the Crown of Castile, which they are. No person may make use of any Indian . . . against his will.[16]

Selected other provisions freed the Indian slaves whose owners did not have legitimate title to them (article 27), reduced the size of large encomiendas and distributed a surplus of Indians among those conquerors who had none (article 32), punished encomenderos who abused Indians by causing them to lose their encomiendas (article 33), limited the number of Indians participating in expeditions to three or four interpreters (article 39), and stated that the Indians, as free vassals of the crown, were to be treated well. "Anyone mistreating them is to be punished according to the laws of Castile" (article 50).[17]

Resistance to the New Laws from the encomenderos was so strong that the crown eventually modified the legislation so that any Indians who voluntarily acquiesced to Spanish rule could not be enslaved. The exception was Indians captured while fighting Spaniards in a "just war." They could become slaves. Idealism had given way to practicality, but another part of the problem was geographical. Enforcing legalities promulgated an ocean and a continent away, laws that ran contrary to reality in central Mexico, was nearly impossible, so in 1549 labor provisions and encomienda were revoked; they never reached northern Mexico and the Pimería Alta.

Similar geographical circumstances occurred a hundred years later in the Pimería Alta when Mexico's governing authority was located hundreds of miles to the south. Because of northern Mexico's remoteness, viceregal and religious edicts, fiats, and royal regulations and laws could be observed or ignored in northern Mexico, depending on the facts of daily life on the frontier. Of course, this situation could not have been known by the thirty-six tribes that "had organized under the name Apache" sometime in the late 1600s or 1700s.[18] Note carefully the words "organized under the name Apache." To me, this means that tribes other than the Chiricahuas might have claimed to be Apaches so that the Chiricahua Apaches would be blamed for the attacks. The colonists and missionaries could also have assumed the marauding Indians were Apaches and so reported. Although the truth may never be known, the Chiricahua Apaches did not cause all the problems, a reasonable conclusion, for no one could be absolutely sure who was who in the midst of the screaming fury, chaos, and confusion of a raid or a battle. And so it went, with the Europeans satisfied most times that Apaches were the culprits responsible for the mounting tolls of death and destruction. Moorhead describes the outcome of this assumption.

> Spain considered the Apaches the most ferocious, vindictive, and irreconcilable . . . [I]t eventually called for the wholesale expatriation of captured Apaches. Even then, the Crown attempted to provide safeguards for the health and welfare of the prisoners of war, but what the Apaches actually experienced was a far cry from what the royal government intended.[19]

In the 1700s some of the Jesuit and Franciscan missionaries took matters into their own hands and devised a plan to control the number of captive Apaches in their missions: selling them. In the early days of this atrocity, because soldiers were still being rewarded with Apaches as slaves, the processes of human trafficking are confusing. Many children were purchased out of the missions, as will be seen, so it is possible that only adults were distributed as booty. Later in the century, as the food supply in missions became insufficient to feed the large numbers of voluntarily surrendered Apaches, Henrique de Grimarest, a high military official, stepped forward with a plan that did not include sales of human beings but was implemented simultaneously. He proposed that the government offer four pesos for each dead Apache or each dead Apache's head. To accomplish this bloody solution to overcrowding, the peaceful Chiricahua volunteers living at the missions/peace establishments were temporarily paroled to kill their tribal members who were emigrating from their encampments toward the missions. The response was astonishing. Many men agreed and left, determined to stop their relatives and friends before they arrived so the amount of rations allotted to each mission resident would not be further reduced.[20] For the first time in the long cultural history of the Chiricahua Apaches, loyalty to one another had been compromised, an unprecedented action and a major cultural shift away from hundred of years of tribal and family allegiances.

Despite this lethal solution the peace establishments/missions were still full, and something more was needed. The answer was not difficult. Spanish administrators recruited the allied Pimas to sell the Apache captives to Tucson area individuals and families wanting slaves. The process got under way quickly. Most of the sales were of men and children because contentious Apache women were the least desirable as servants. If the Pimas could not sell their female prisoners, they simply killed them, believing there would be no retribution from any of the authorities.[21] Whether murdering the Apache women was an order from the Spanish officials or was the Pimas' own solution is not clear. If the latter, the action had to be endorsed by someone in power and concurred with by mission administrators.

One of the Franciscans on the frontier, Diego Miguel Bringas de Manzaneda y Encinas, OFM, known simply as Father Bringas, praised the Pimas for their cooperation.[22] In a long letter dated March 13, 1796, to the commandante general, Father Bringas described the fidelity of the Pimas, their means of sustenance, and "another activity which is all the more necessary in that it consists in the diminution of our enemies, the Apache. They take Apache prisoners to the nearby missions."[23] In this long epistle Father Bringas understandably avoided elaborating on what was done with the Indians at the missions.

Nor did he, in any manner, voice objections to what he must have known was occurring. By acquiescing in the sales of Apaches to local Spanish Roman Catholic families, this priest could have sincerely trusted that the receiving families would bring them to the altar of Roman Catholicism. Some of the purchasers acted in good faith, as shown by the 1798 census of Arizpe, Mexico. Fifty-two former Apaches captives between the ages of three and twenty had been distributed to twenty-five Spanish households, and according to James Officer, "sacramental registers from communities in northern Sonora reveal that most, if not all, the Indians who wound up in Hispanic homes during the last dozen years of the eighteenth century became Catholic converts."[24] Without the complete figures, however, it is impossible to reach an accurate conclusion regarding the number of families who followed through on their obligation to Christianize the slaves.

In the Tubac/Tumacácori/Guévavi region, data were also being compiled regarding Apaches in the 1700s. It should be kept in mind that Apache was a generic identifier and not necessarily correct. These Jesuit and Franciscan records omit the captives' tribal names, as the men, women, and children were immediately baptized upon reaching the mission or presidio. Some were in better physical condition than others; several perished soon after baptism. One very important caveat must be explained before reading the abbreviated list of names. I subscribe to Kessell's statement, "'Godfather' is the term used to indicate purchaser,"[25] though others may argue differently.[26] In the sample that follows, it may be assumed that godparents were the purchasers unless otherwise noted; they became the owners of the Apache slaves.

The information below is taken from Mission 2000, a database publicly available on the internet and credited to the Diocese of Tucson, Arizona.[27]

In the Jesuit Era

Gertrudis, age five or six, was baptized at Guévavi on August 13, 1741, ostensibly by an interim Basque Jesuit named Ildefonso de la Peña. Soon afterward this priest was deemed unsuitable for mission work, reason unknown, by Fathers Keller and Sedelmayr, and did not stay. Gertrudis's godfather was Miguel (Miguelito) Díaz, a longtime resident of the San

Luis valley. Married to María de Pilar Figueroa, they fled to Terrenate (a presidio) at the news of the Pima uprising in 1751. No further information is available about Gertrudis.

José Luis, age five or six, was baptized at Guévavi on April 22, 1746, by Joseph Garrucho, SJ. He was purchased for Nicholás Romero by Juan Timotheo de Robles. No further information is available about José Luis or Romero. Father Garrucho, however, was implicated by Pima revolt leader Luis as one of the causes for the rebellion and had to defend himself later in a Mexico City court because of the accusations. Under his supervision, Pimas built a church at Guévavi, his guidance kept the mission ranch at Tubac producing, and he got along well with settlers and other neighbors. He endured longer than any other priest at Guévavi but was expelled from the frontier in 1767 with all other Jesuits. He died in 1785 at a European monastery.

Carlos José is an enigma. The son of a non-Christian Apache father, whose name was not recorded, the boy was baptized on May 23, 1748, at Sonoita, probably by Father Garrucho. No further information about Carlos José is available.

María Michaela, the infant daughter of a non-Christian Apache father, was baptized on either September 29, 1748, or October 29, 1748—different dates are provided—at Guévavi by Father Garrucho, who wrote, "I solemnly baptized Maria, daughter of Ignacio and Juana Tuburi-ubi. Her godfather was Don Joachin Gonzales Barrientos," who died on November 21, 1751, in the Pima revolt. Maria's fate is unknown.

Xavier Beldarrain, a young boy who lived at Tubac, was baptized by Jesuit Keller at Guévavi on December 8, 1753. He was the last of twenty-eight children baptized that day and was subsequently purchased by Juan Tomás Beldarrain, who became the first commander of the presidio of Tubac. Beldarrain's authoritative position at Tubac likely accounts for the notation describing the boy's residence. After a long involvement with several missions on the frontier, Beldarrain died from a Seri Indian arrow wound on September 7, 1759, supposedly while confessing a dying Pima during the heat of an uprising, and was buried beneath the altar steps at Guévavi. Xavier disappeared from the rolls.

José Ignacio, an eight-year-old boy, was baptized on February 27, 1754, at Guévavi by Jesuit Pauer. José Ignacio's father was named as Francisco Figueroa, but his godparents were Juan Felipe and Juana

Romero; she is also listed as the wife of Juan Miguel Martínez. No further information is available about José Ignacio or about his father, who carried a Spanish name. Father Pauer supervised the natives who built churches at Tumacácori and Sonoitac. He served many years at Guévavi beginning in 1753, at Suamca, and at San Ignacio, but was expelled in 1767. He died in Cadiz, Spain, on January 6, 1770, from the "rigor of expulsion and imprisonment."

Four children were brought to Tubac on March 28, 1754, probably survivors of a battle. Juan Ramón was baptized twice that day, once by a lay individual named Joachin Félix Díaz, possibly a soldier, with unblessed water, and the second time with holy oil by Father Pauer. This unusual activity indicates an acute medical situation, so serious that it had to be addressed immediately before the priest could arrive from Guévavi. Miguel Gabriel was also baptized that day by the same soldier with unblessed water. Father Pauer arrived later and administered the holy oil. Juan Lorenzo, the third boy, was also baptized twice. A girl, María Francisca, listed as Nijorita—from an unknown tribe, sold by other Indians to Tubac—was the fourth member of this small bunch and also baptized twice. There is no indication whether these children lived or died or how they arrived at Tubac. The circumstances suggested that all were in an emergency condition because of injuries; hence, the sacrament could be administered by any Roman Catholic individual with honorable intentions, placing the children in good stead should they perish before the priest reached the presidio.

On November 9, 1758, Father Pauer posthumously baptized a female at Guévavi named María de Luz, who was the slave of don Ignacio Díaz del Carpio. María's godparents were Santiago de la Cruz and Ignacia Tapia. Her owner, Díaz del Carpio, had been born in Chihuahua, Mexico, and was a lieutenant in the army stationed at Janos, Mexico. He was forty-seven years old and owned ten horses and two mules. This situation bears close resemblance to the policy of rewarding military service with Apache slaves. Nothing more is known about María.

María Loreta Romero, the infant daughter of her owner, Nicholás Romero, was baptized by a German Jesuit, Miguel Gerstner, at Guévavi on March 21, 1761. Romero had been buying children since at least 1746, when he purchased José Luis, described earlier. María had already been baptized with water by don Ignacio Díaz del Carpio before Gerstner administered the sacrament. Romero was a witness to the investigation of the Pima revolt, owned many ranch properties in the region, and moved to Tubac as a widower. It is unknown whether he took María Loreta with him, but information reveals that a María Loreta Romero died on August 15, 1762, in Buena Vista, possibly at one of Romero's properties. She was buried in Guévavi's cemetery. In the Tubac census of 1767 Romero is listed as having three daughters and three sons living in his household. Father Gerstner, a man who was continually ill, administered Guévavi for sixteen months, leaving on May 25, 1761. He was expelled in 1767 and kept under house arrest in a Spanish monastery.

Hernando Ignacio Manuel Mesa, whom Domingo de Mesa owned, was eight years old when baptized by Father Gerstner at Guévavi on June 4, 1760. In this case, Hernando's owner was different from his godfather, a soldier named Manuel Gonzales stationed at Tubac in 1752.

In the Franciscan Era

María Cathalina, about eight or ten years old at the time of her baptism, was captured by Anza, owned by him, and baptized by Gaspar de Clemente, OFM, at Tumacácori on February 13, 1774. Her godmother was Ana María Atondo, a widow and resident of Tubac. Father Clemente wrote that he advised the widow of her spiritual and other obligations. There is no further information available.

José Xavier, seven years old, was captured by Anza at the same time, was owned by him, baptized by Father Clemente on the same day at Tumacácori, and had the same godmother. Father Clemente was at Tumacácori by November 1772. Along with his colleague, Bartolomé Ximeno, OFM, they supervised Indians building a wall around the entire mission complex, had the Calabazas church roofed with native labor, and designated a consecrated cemetery there. Father Clemente's health failed, causing him to leave the frontier early in 1775 at the age of thirty, for the Franciscan college at Querétaro, where he stayed for about fifteen years and then disappeared from view.

Of undetermined age, Antonio was baptized on July 19, 1774, at Tumacácori by two friars, Fathers Gil de Bernabé and Moreno. María Emerenciana Romero was the individual's godmother, as well as the wife of José Ignacio Sosa. She had been raised at Guévavi (perhaps she was indigenous?), but she and her husband might have been living at Tumacácori at the time Antonio was baptized. Father Gil de Bernabé arrived at Guévavi in mid-May 1768, among the first Franciscans on the frontier. He became ill, was transferred in the spring of 1771, but returned to the area and Tumacácori by September. He left Tumacácori in the winter of 1771–72 for the Franciscan college at Querétaro and became its father president. Seris murdered him on March 7, 1773, in an uprising on Tuburón Island, where he had established a mission a year earlier. His body was exhumed in October 1773 and reburied in Ures. Father Moreno joined Clemente at Tumacácori for about a year, taking part in the mass at Tubac on January 8, 1774, for Anza before he departed the area to discover a route to Alta California. His wife supervised the children's baptisms the next month. Father Moreno left Tumacácori early in 1775 to be stationed at Caborca with Pedro Font, OFM. Under their supervision the church at Pitiquito was built. Father Moreno was transferred to the Yuma mission on the Colorado River in 1780, and Yumas beheaded him in 1781.

The infant Manuel de la Trinidad was brought to Tumacácori on May 19, 1799, and baptized immediately because he was very ill. Narciso Gutiérrez, OFM, issued the sacrament to this baby from a non-Christian family while Dolores Villelas held the child as he received the holy water. She became his godmother.

Mathias Zúñiga, the son of a non-Christian Indian, was five or six years old at the time of his baptism by Father Gutiérrez at Tumacácori on February 24, 1800. His godparents are listed as José Pineda and Mariana López. José was born in Arivaca and raised at Guévavi; he died at Tumacácori on March 20, 1804. He was not married to Mathias's godmother, about whom nothing is known. At age twenty-nine, Father Gutiérrez arrived in Tumacácori on July 10, 1794, and served twenty-six years there, longer than any other Franciscan. He died at Tumacácori on December 13, 1820, was buried in the Jesuit church on the grounds, exhumed two years later, and reburied in the Franciscan church's sanctuary on the side facing the altar beside his colleague, Balthasar Carrillo, OFM.

Pedro Antonio Galindo, about seven years old, was baptized by Father Gutiérrez on September 24, 1802, and then sold to his owner/godfather, Pedro Galindo, at Tumacácori. No further information is available.

Mathias Madorran, about eight or nine years old at the time of his death on July 29, 1803, was buried by Father Gutiérrez in the children's section of the cemetery at Tumacácori. No cause of death was noted and no other information recorded.

José María Dolores Narbona was about four years old when Father Gutiérrez baptized him at Tumacácori on September 15, 1804. He was the son of a non-Christian Indian and sold to Antonio Narbona and his wife, Isabel, residents of Tumacácori. About one year later an unknown epidemic struck the mission and José died. He was buried in the cemetery.

Estevan Mallen, a thirteen-year-old boy, was baptized at Tumacácori by Father Gutiérrez on May 4, 1807, after having been instructed in Roman Catholic doctrine. He specifically requested that his name be Estevan. His godfather was Ramón Ríos, married to Gertrudis Borboa; they lived at Tumacácori. Estevan's godmother was Manuela Gonzales, the widow of Lucas Miranda; she lived at Tubac. Estevan married Dolores Gonzales; their infant son, Leonardo, died on November 21, 1813. Estevan himself died on November 21, 1816, at the age of twenty-two. He asked for and received extreme unction before death and was buried at Tumacácori. His wife Dolores died at the age of twenty-four on December 12, 1816. She received the holy sacraments before death and was also buried in the Tumacácori cemetery.

Cayetano, a child of about three or four years old, was baptized by Father Gutiérrez on November 18, 1808, at Tumacácori. His godparents were María del Pilar and Juan Legarra. He had been sold to the mission by non-Christian Indians. No further information was available.

⚶

A cursory review of similar situations in other area missions during the Jesuit and Franciscan years reveals much of the same. Below is a random sample of those activities.

In the Jesuit Era

Nicholas Turaqui of Magdalena became the godfather for two girls in 1708. On April 8, Lucía, about seven years old, was baptized by Father Campos. On December 3 of that year he also baptized Teresa. There is no further information about these children. Father Campos became a Jesuit at age fifteen. He began his ministry at San Ignacio in 1693 at the age of twenty-four but was removed by his superiors for reasons not listed. He resided at Guévavi for a time, left there on April 9, 1722, and returned on May 24, 1723. He may have been the first to record the name of Tubac in 1726. As Kino's close friend, they traveled together and proselytized all across the frontier. Campos died on July 1, 1737.

Rosa Micaela was one of sixteen children and one adult baptized by Father Campos on August 6, 1727, at San Ignacio. No further information available.

At San Ignacio on October 31, 1743, Gaspar Stiger, SJ, baptized María Bárbara, who was owned and raised by Juan de Villa. Her godparents were Xavier Samaniego and Magdalena Germán. Father Stiger entered the Jesuits on October 9, 1725, and traveled to New Spain five years later. After being stationed at Bac and Guévavi, he moved to San Ignacio, where he stayed twenty-five years. He died on April 24, 1762, and was buried in the sanctuary in front of the main altar on the gospel side, next to Father Pauer.

Chepa, fourteen years old, was baptized on June 21, 1744, at San Ignacio by Father Stiger. Chepa was owned and raised by don Miguel de Mendoza Castellanos, a lieutenant in the jurisdiction, who died in 1748, cause of death not listed.

Ignacio, an infant and probably injured, was captured during an early morning attack by a Sergeant Barrios while hunting Apaches near Suamca on August 29, 1738. Father Keller baptized the baby immediately, naming the child after himself; Ignacio died soon after.

María Guadalupe, an infant, was baptized on October 22, 1760, at Suamca by Diego José Barrera, SJ. Her godfather was Juan José, an Indian ally who was a lieutenant in the jurisdiction, the mayor of Suamca who became the governor in 1763. Father Barrera was assigned to Suamca after Father Keller's death in 1759. He stayed until the Jesuit expulsion in 1767 and was imprisoned for more than ten years in Spain. He died there on March 2, 1782, at the age of fifty-three years.

In the Franciscan Era

Agustín Ignacio was about three years old at the time of his baptism on September 9, 1787, in Arizpe by Ignacio Ballemilla, OFM. His godparents were Manuel Antonio de la Azuela and María Petra García. No further information is available.

Celedonio, a four- or five-year-old boy, was baptized on March 3, 1772, at Tubutama by Esteban de Salazar, OFM. Celedonio had been purchased by Vicente Cojo, an Indian living at Tubutama, from Pápago Indian sellers. Father Salazar was one of the original Franciscans on the frontier in 1768. He was initially assigned to Ures and by 1769 was in Tubutama, where he stayed until at least 1772.

৩৪

A sample of the deaths and burials of Apaches at Janos, their names, the priests' names, and names of their owners, are listed below.

Alonso, an adult Apache, died on June 25, 1723, during an unidentified epidemic after having been baptized that same day and buried by Jesuit Bernardo Aris Navarrete in the Janos cemetery with a "low cross." No explanation was provided. This epidemic claimed the lives of many adult Apaches, some of whom were slaves. They all were buried in the Janos cemetery.

On November 3, 1724, an Apache infant named Benito, of unknown parentage but owned by Antonio Bezerra Nieto, died and was buried by a Jesuit priest named Tomás Antonio Bezerra Nieto, possibly a relative of the baby's owner.

Later that month, on November 16, Jesuit Nieto buried Jacinta, the child of Apache slaves owned by Cayetano Madrid, a soldier who also owned ten horses and one mule.

Four days later the same priest buried Ignacio, the child slave of the well-known military officer Juan Bautista de Anza Sr., who was subsequently killed by Apaches near Suamca in a battle on May 8, 1740.

On January 30, 1738, an Apache woman named María died and was buried by Jesuit Francisco Xavier Ponce de León inside the presidio chapel, beneath the choir loft. She was Marcial Gómez's slave; he was a soldier at the Janos presidio who also owned ten horses and one mule.

On April 24, 1741, an adult Apache woman was baptized by Jesuit Simón de Arceo. At that time she was the slave of Lucas de Abesia and worked for him until July 17, 1748, when she died during an epidemic and was buried by the same priest.

On December 20, 1741, the same priest buried Mariana, another slave of the well-known Lucas de Abecia, who paid for the burial in advance.

On April 2, 1743, the child María Antonia died and was buried by the Jesuit priest Francisco Xavier Ponce de León. She was the daughter of a mulatto slave named Joseph Miguel and an Apache woman named Antonia. Her godmother was María Antonia del Río.

On July 23, 1748, María Ana, the Apache slave of an officer named Lt. Francisco Elías González, died during an epidemic and was given an "ecclesiastic burial" by José Montaño, a Jesuit priest.

Another death during that same epidemic, on July 28, 1748, was that of María Francisca, an adult Apache who was the slave of a blacksmith named Gerónimo. She was buried without sacraments because the Jesuit priest, José Montaño, was absent.

On May 25, 1759, an Apache slave named Antonio was killed in a raid by Apaches. A note from the priest, José Anselmo García de Noriega, SJ, stated, "The holy sacraments were not administered because he perished at the hands of the enemy Indians of the Apache nation." The wording of this note can be confusing, but it probably means that Antonio died before the sacraments could be administered.

On February 13, 1764, an Apache child slave named Francisco died and was buried by Father García de Noriega in the baptistery of the presidio's chapel. Francisco may have been an orphan and recently brought to Janos. No owners are listed.

᠙

This small sample from selected areas is proof of the terrible event that occurred all across the frontier in the eighteenth century. From this evidence we know that slavery, which Spanish law prohibited, existed extra-legally; no secret there. We know that the military, officers and enlisted men, were rewarded with captured slaves as a supplement to their meager income. Chiricahua Apaches were deported to central Mexico and Cuba as slaves. Quite a few Indian allies and friendly Chiricahua Apaches supported Spanish goals, including restricting the number of emigrants to the peace establishments, by killing them. What we do not know from the written record is exactly how or whether the Jesuits and Franciscans benefited from the sale of human beings to godfathers, godmothers, patrons, the military, and others who would promise to raise them as Christians. The obvious first assumption would be that the new owners of indigenous slaves paid the missionaries for them in cash or supplies or commodities. That would not be a surprise, especially since slaves were freely and openly awarded to military personnel, a practice that had been occurring and endorsed for years. Second, many missions were in dire straits, needing additional monies and supplies to meet the dual goals of their obligations. They took their responsibilities seriously and were willing to risk their lives to meet them. A paradox was thus created.

By definition, a paradox is a situation that exhibits contradictory tendencies. As more and more tribal peoples sought protection and shelter at the missions after intensified military actions, pressures increased on the missions' already scarce resources, and innovative measures became crucial for the survival of the missions.

Practically speaking, an infusion of revenue, cash, or credit from the sales would allow the missionaries to continue their work on the frontier without the constant worries about shortfalls. With enough funds or matériel at hand, they could keep the missions operating in order to save more souls, some of whom they could sell to keep the missions functioning to save more souls whom they could sell, and so on. Even though there is no unassailable proof of this activity, nothing that can be corroborated, it is not an improbable situation, given many of the illegal and immoral conditions already existing on the colonial frontier. A Spanish attorney on the frontier, Galindo Navarro, summed up the situation on December 9, 1796, writing, "There is absolutely no other way to save these captives from inevitable death if there's no profit to their captors."[28] Did the missionaries interpret this statement as a way to save souls by forcing salvation through slavery upon the indigenes? Although the issue is murky, nothing substantive has emerged to suggest, much less reveal, that they opposed human trafficking. No objections were documented by officials or anyone else to at least give the impression that the clergy refused to hand over the newly baptized Apaches and other Indians to purchasers. The silence is deafening.

Identity Theft and Enslavement

౪ TWO RELATED THEMES OF THIS BOOK, IDENTITY THEFT AND ENSLAVEMENT, comprise a significant core of the Chiricahua Apache experience on the Spanish colonial frontier. These destructive events were deliberate; baptism by the Jesuits and Franciscans ordinarily occurred first before certain priests sold the captives into slavery. Apaches with Christian names were a guarantee to the purchaser that the individual had been put on the path to salvation and civilization, a route that was to be continued under the supervision of the new owner.

Two hundred years before any of this tragedy took place, migrating Athapascans reached northern Mexico, around 1450, according to Deni J. Seymour.[1] On arrival they were a somewhat different group than those who had originally left the Arctic Circle, having experienced human and cultural exchanges along the southward journey. The newcomers, mixed now with other tribal peoples, learned to adapt to the desert environment that was so unlike the cold north, made friends and enemies of local tribes already established, continued to trade customs and people, and settled into a comfortable routine of sharing desert resources. During times of drought, however, raiding and fighting for scarce foods and water broke out, and then the friends became adversaries.

Enslavement of enemies during these battles was a fact of life. Not always victorious in intertribal warfare, the Apaches themselves also lost tribal members in conflicts, so slavery was a familiar concept when the Spanish arrived and practiced it on the colonial frontier. Being forcibly removed from the land Ussen had expected them to preserve and protect, being sent to Mexico City and Cuba to labor, and being sold as slaves in their own homelands was a new experience, though. This eventually produced an unprecedented situation, especially in the late 1700s: hundreds of Chiricahua Apaches surrendering and subjecting themselves to Spanish authority for safety and to avoid deportation. Now they were imprisoned side by side with friends and relatives who had been captured during hostilities and confined at the same missions.

Part of that extraordinary predicament was identity theft, the consequences of which are still obvious today, nearly four hundred years later. Several Chiricahua Apaches families carry Spanish surnames and are Roman Catholics who worship at St. Joseph's Mission on the Mescalero Apache Reservation. Many of these descendants are related over time to at least two sets of the compromised Chiricahuas: those who professed Christianity in the mission settings and those whose owners kept their promise to continue converting the Indians to Roman Catholicism. The fate of the Apaches whose owners ignored their pledge and the others who were transferred to Cuba is unknown.

Given the incredible human instinct to survive, an interesting possibility arises regarding the religious requirements at the missions: deception. Were the Chiricahuas true "converts" or was this situation more apparent than real? Many Indians from various tribal backgrounds appeared to accept Roman Catholicism as a first step to becoming integrated into the Spaniards' community.[2] Axtell noted the possibility of misleading behavior, however, stating, "The Indians ensured the survival of the native culture by taking on the protective coloration of the invaders' religion . . . This brand of Christianity often lay very lightly on the surface of their lives."[3] Two Jesuits offered another clue to certain indigenes' insincerity. Father Segesser wrote in a letter, "Indians do not come to Christian service when they do not see the maize pot boiling,"[4] and Father Sedlmayr wrote, "When they [the Indians] say they want to be Christians . . . it usually means they want a horse, clothing, knife, or cloth."[5]

Although neither Axtell, Segesser, nor Sedlmayr mentions the Chiricahua Apaches by name, one of their individual and tribal characteristics traits was pragmatism. In other words, in challenging situations they did what they had to do to either reach their goals or, much more seriously, survive. Thus, the Apaches' acceptance of Roman Catholicism was either genuine or simply pragmatic lip-service pronouncements that negotiated and facilitated food, shelter, and survival.

Griffen reported that the Janos Chiricahuas' "attitude toward Christianity was one of aloofness and indifference," which was demonstrated in the fact that the mission residents also "learned many new vices, including card games, obscene language, songs and dances, concubinage, and a host of other improprieties and indecent customs" from the local residents.[6] Understandably, the allure of the latter far outweighed the former.

By the time the Apaches engaged in this type of raucous behavior, however, they had gone through the process of losing their unique personal identity by being baptized and acquiring Hispanicized names. In other words, through baptism their tribal and ancestral affiliation had been deliberately stolen and replaced by strange sounding words that had no meaning.[7]

It is obvious that the Jesuits and Franciscans certainly did not consider baptism to be identity theft. In the Roman Catholic belief system, the sacrament of baptism washes away the original sin all human beings are believed to have been born with, thus producing a clean slate onto which the tenets of Christianity may be permanently etched, starting with a new name.

Thus, erasing the sacredness of indigenous names, family ties, and tribal affiliation by sprinkling water and muttering a few incomprehensible words was an essential step toward Christianization and signaled to a potential purchaser that the baptized individual was now ready to begin becoming a responsible member of civilized society. In renaming the natives, the men of God created an avalanche of destruction in the indigenes' personal lives that disrupted personal and cultural unity with the past, severing a connection that joined an individual with his ancestral history and his tribe and robbing him of his integrity.

The priests' blatant dishonesty in conducting this ceremony occurred each time they recorded names and raw numbers of those baptized in ledgers, notebooks, or letters and then submitted the documents to the Spanish authorities as proof of their success. The higher the numbers, the more impressed religious and secular superiors were, and that reflected favorably on the priest responsible for producing the data. As these missionaries were not fools, they must have known their actions were spurious and could be misleading to those reading the report. The Jesuits and Franciscans conducted mass baptisms nonetheless, cavalierly listing the numbers—some may have been exaggerated—with full knowledge that most of the adults lacked comprehension of the holy rite. Yes, the data they generated lied about the sincerity of the intent, and their immoral behavior is inexcusable.

An act similar in procedures to baptism occurred at an Apache child's birth. Ancient midwifery practices called for a medicine woman to wash and bless a newborn with tepid water immediately after a baby's entrance into the world. As she prayed, squirting the water over the newborn was believed to be very beneficial because of the natural medicinal properties it contained. If no water was available, or if the Chiricahuas were being pursued by an enemy, the healer's sputum was an accepted substitute. After the short washing ceremony, the infant was dried with grass, soft moss, or a cloth. The Apache midwife sprinkled sacred pollen over the newborn and placed the baby in a cradleboard, constructed in advance by the mother, grandmother, or a female relative who said appropriate prayers for the baby's welfare and long life during each phase of creating the carrier. Naming the child was accomplished through a ceremony that was held immediately after delivery or, depending on the circumstances, could be postponed until a more appropriate time.

In contrast to a Christian name, an Apache infant's name was often impermanent and could change several times during a person's lifetime. For example, as a child of nine or ten years, a girl may have been skilled in making dolls, and her birth name would be changed at that age to reflect the attribute. As she grew into adulthood, she might have been exceptionally generous, so the childhood name would be traded then for one that told the world how giving she was. In her senior years she might gain a reputation as a kindly grandmother and would then take on another name that identified her as such.[8]

Unlike a baptismal name, cultural taboos were also associated with an Apache's name. Injunctions against certain actions involved with a name indicate value in not speaking a name. One of Opler's informants told him, "The name is very valuable. Children are taught not to call a person's name when they meet him. [If someone calls a name] . . . the person would then be under obligation to do anything for another . . . [Otherwise] it is considered very impolite."[9] A few contemporary but traditional Apaches are still influenced by the age-old customs related specifically to the use of a deceased person's name. For example, Elbys Naiche Hugar, a great-granddaughter of Cochise, has her own thoughts about it. "Your dead relative may be very busy doing something important where he is and when he hears you speak his name, he'll be interrupted. He might not like that."[10]

Another example of identity theft occurred through European land appropriation. For example, in the Chiricahua Apache belief system cultural and spiritual geography were extremely significant. As Ussen had caused them to halt in northern Mexico, their physical surroundings symbolized Ussen's specific desire for the Apaches. In their eyes this wish was one of the pillars of their existence and became a significant component of their total culture. The names they applied to places within the area anchored their lives to the region, to the site Ussen had chosen for them, and to a spot where their blood and bones could be buried. Thus, naming sites across the landscape produced a spiritual relationship with the land and maintained an eternal and inviolate connection between themselves and their god. Investing the earth with spirituality caused a specific location to have more than a physical identity; it was sacred.

In a supreme expression of disdain, the missionaries deliberately built religious complexes, beginning with simple ramadas, directly over many of the indigenes' sacred sites, desecrating what had been honored and revered. Intimidated immediately by this audacity, some of the more timid indigenous tribes soon accepted the Jesuits' presence despite their shamans' warnings to the contrary. Not to be overlooked by any means is the arrogant application of the biblical permission for dominion through the policy of reducción/congregación that vacated Indian lands and opened them for habitation by Spanish pioneers. These settlers further altered the sacred landscape to suit themselves. The natives were overwhelmed.

Incredibly, if the priests sincerely believed "they were . . . continuing the work of Christ and his disciples," as Reff quotes others as concluding, the missionaries' pathological disregard for the consequences of their actions may be viewed by some as sacrilegious.[11] In an attempt to understand their immorality, however, let us take a look at who these men were as human beings rather than supposedly pious men of God.

The frontier Jesuits and Franciscans represented a full spectrum of humanity, ranging from noble characteristics to hurtful personality flaws. Some men were pleasant, some irritable. Some were strict, some flexible. Some were kindly disposed, some rigid. Some were sympathetic to the indigenes, some callous. Their conduct toward the natives varied from man to man and mission to mission as they pursued their own agendas based on quantitative goals rather than qualitative achievements. This difference in purpose is fundamental to the conflicting mind sets that collided on the colonial frontier. Despite their individuality, the Jesuits and Franciscans all had one trait in common: without thinking twice, they blindly believed their efforts were for the Indians' own good and they, as agents of the cross and crown, represented the only true way to salvation—Christianity. Baptizing, enslaving, and, in time, selling the Indians were the preferred and expeditious routes to saving their souls, they concluded. In so doing, however, each of these religious men was guilty of committing the very sins his Roman Catholicism prohibited in Christian thought and action.

Along with regimentation and forced labor, the conditions of mission life promoted cultural assimilation processes. Griffen wrote that documents from the region showed "the missionaries usually made little effort to keep members of distinct Indian ethnic groups separate . . . Whether this practice was part of . . . policy or not . . . it does exemplify the great mixing of peoples . . . during the colonial period."[12] The close proximity of differing tribal peoples in a confining setting brought the incarcerated groups into contact under difficult circumstances. It would not be unreasonable to assume that some individuals gravitated toward each other in an attempt to survive their predicament, and again alliances were made, customs exchanged, and people joined, causing a physical and cultural mix of populations who had already suffered identity theft. One benefit to the priests of the indigenes' close contact within the mission setting was an increase in the number of children. Some of these babies no doubt reflected a blending of ethnic backgrounds that would positively influence sales. The Apaches had such a bad reputation that a child of mixed parentage would likely be easier to sell than a full Apache.

To further complicate identities, the Spaniards conveniently labeled many indigenous Apache regardless of their tribal affiliation. Griffen wrote, "The term 'Apache' apparently was employed when the priest could not identify the Indians by ethnic group, judging from the high frequency of its use in baptisms of children of unknown parents."[13] Clearly many were the descendants of the Athapascans but others were not, as Griffen noted.

> The first 30 years or so of the 1700s show them [the original native populations of the region] near the end of their existence as distinctive cultural systems or societies. After this period . . . of the uncontrolled native groups, only the Apaches survived and they became the sole occupants of the non-Spanish held territory.[14]

Stern believed non-Indians were also included within the surviving Apache groups: blacks and black racial mixtures, military malcontents and misfits, transients, vagrants, and former members of other frontier Indian tribes.[15] It is possible that some of these voluntarily joined the Chiricahua Apaches, went to war with their new comrades, had been captured, became prisoners of the Spanish, and were sold, incarcerated, killed, enslaved, or deported to Cuba. Interest in receiving the exiles was rising in Cuba. Cuban citizens, especially those living in Havana, "petitioned to receive one or more Indians [and non-Indians] with demand seeming to exceed available supply," Archer wrote, adding that

> the Christian spirit was notably lacking as the primary interest in the Indians, however, although all letters requesting them made promises regarding education and religious training. Unfortunately, the requests more often than not went on to give reasons why a certain family needed an extra "slave," due to the pressure of large families, small fixed incomes, or for sundry other reasons. [16]

This is not surprising, but who could have imagined that the men of God, the Jesuits and the Franciscans, would break all the moral and legal maxims and become involved in human trafficking? Certainly they were aware of their renown as honorable men, and surely they were familiar with well-known legalities that addressed treatment of the indigenes. Since the New Laws of 1542 predated the missionaries' entrance into northern Mexico, one may assume that they were versed in its provisions and prohibitions. And still they abused the natives. During the early 1700s, while the missionaries were occupied with their work in northern Mexico, the Reglamento of 1729 expressly forbid distributing captured Apaches as the spoils of war. Also under this regulation the prisoners were to be sent to the vicinity of Mexico City, where the viceroy, not the Jesuits in Sonora, would decide their fate. The first evidence of activity is recorded ten years later, in 1739, when an Apache chief and thirteen of his followers in Texas were transported to Mexico City after spending more than one year in jail in San Antonio. Moorhead reported that "no other Apaches captured in the northern provinces were sent to the viceregal capital during the next three decades,"[17] which implies that the captives continued to be given out illegally to military families as rewards for service.

In 1772 a new reglamento prohibited abuse of Indian prisoners of war and reiterated that they be transferred to Mexico City and subjected to the viceroy's wishes, a law that the Franciscans should have obeyed. Seven years later, in 1779, a royal order required that all surrendered Indians, regardless of tribal background, were to be treated humanely; nothing stipulated that they be deported from their homelands to Mexico City or anywhere else for distribution or to be sold locally as slaves. On the contrary the order demanded that the military officials prevent Apache captives from being treated as property.

One year after the Instructions of 1786 were issued, Comm. Gen. Jacobo Ugarte reported that his officers had sent captured Apaches to the jails and workhouses across the frontier, but most of these prisoners were women and children. Some children were sent to the Real de Álamos in Sonora where they would be distributed to private homes whose families were expected to feed, clothe, educate, and Christianize the children. The viceroy approved and announced that he would send the male prisoners out of the country so they would never again be able to practice their traditional raiding life-styles. This was the first official mention of deportation to Cuba.

Because so many cunning, fearless, and desperate Apaches had escaped from the marches to Mexico City through "Spanish inadequacies in methods of handling prisoners," one year later the viceroy put his pronouncement into practice and sent many captured Apaches to

Veracruz, where they would be shipped to Havana, never to return to northern Mexico.[18] "By a royal order of April 11, 1799, this procedure became mandatory," and then "the Crown ruled in 1803 that all Apache prisoners would be sent to Havana."[19]

Deadly diseases as well as chronic debilities accompanied these Apache prisoners along the overland routes. In 1787 Veracruz seaport authorities reported that of the sixty-one who had arrived from Sonora via Mexico City the previous November, only twenty-eight were alive to board the ship for Havana. Plans to ship enslaved Apaches to the island continued for at least a decade, as reports show that of seventy-one Apaches arriving in Mexico City on December 26, 1797, only nineteen were well enough to sail. Smallpox, an undiagnosed ailment noted as "putrid fever," the pestilential conditions of incarceration, and a variety of contagious diseases contracted before or during the death marches were to blame for the fatalities. Moorhead reported that

> in 1739 and 1797–98, more than half of the Apache prisoners died in Mexico City and Vera Cruz, largely from disease and malnutrition . . . The sordid details of the procedure—strict confinement, forced labor, family separation, and the absence of provisions for eventual release—suggest an actual practice, if not a deliberate policy, of sheer genocide.[20]

And so, the possibility of genocide has come to our attention. This is a word with meaning so abominable and so distressing that its definition is often misunderstood, is often used loosely, or even hinted at to describe many crimes against humanity. For example, while not using the word, Archer wrote, "From the percentages of women and children sent into exile, it becomes apparent that the Spanish planned the complete removal of offending Indian populations and [their] potential for raising new generations of warriors."[21]

On the surface, this sounds like genocide, but before any conclusion can be reached about the veracity of accusations, a definition of genocide must be understood. Ward Churchill has pointed out that at a 1948 Draft Convention of the United Nations, genocide was defined as "destruction of a group" and as "preventing its preservation and development."[22] Granted, this is a very broad statement that was developed under totally different circumstances than those that existed hundreds of years previously, yet the actions leading to genocide or the act of genocide itself are ageless.

Under the above definitions, it is undeniable that the Jesuits and Franciscans were guilty of genocide insofar as the Chiricahua Apaches are concerned. Identity theft and enslavement are unmistakable proof of the priests' intent to destroy and prevent the Apaches' continuation as a people. In this effort the men of God were supported by Galindo Navarro, an auditor and lawyer on the colonial frontier who endorsed the missionaries' use of Pima allies to sell Apache captives. As he wrote on December 9, 1796,

> the [Pimas] will kill the adult women for whom they can expect no payment . . . It is just and fitting that we assist them . . . in the sale and barter of . . . prisoners . . . so far as possible against our common enemy [Chiricahua Apaches]. . . . [I]nstead of forbidding this it is proper to tolerate and even to encourage in the future . . . The frontier captains should not prevent [the Pimas] from selling or trading . . . hostile Apaches."[23]

The haunting question is why, in violation of all that was holy in their lives, would these pious men sell, or cause to be sold, other human beings? There are no recorded answers for this inexplicable and inexcusable action. With careful thought, though, a framework of sorts may be placed around the Jesuits' and Franciscans' attempted genocidal murder of the Chiricahua Apaches. Calling upon the United Nations' definitions for guidance, one may conclude that the missionaries and their accomplices, using identity theft and enslavement, deliberately attempted to destroy the Chiricahua Apache culture, thus preventing its preservation and development.

To begin this framework, we would initially acknowledge that the paltry sum of 250 to 350 pesos annually paid to the priests was often much less than what was frequently needed to meet a mission's basic needs. With this small amount a priest was expected to accomplish miracles at his facilities, including filling the human needs of the indigenes, procuring supplies of all types, tending livestock, and providing religious services to the surrounding communities of natives and Europeans.

Occasionally there was not enough food for the number of dependent mission Indians, a situation that occurred during both the Jesuit and Franciscan eras. These circumstances became especially acute after the Instructions of 1786 were issued, and more and more Chiricahua Apaches voluntarily surrendered themselves at the missions to avoid death during intensive military campaigns. At that time the food shortage was so serious that some Apaches, already part of the mission setting, agreed to kill other Apaches before they reached the missions.

An increase in funds to keep the missions afloat was thus imperative. Money received through selling Indians into slavery would definitely improve the precarious situation. With cash or credit on hand, the Jesuits and Franciscans could purchase meat, vegetables, fruits, and other foodstuffs from the local ranchers and farmers to meet the basic needs of the natives living in the mission setting and those soon to arrive. Without enough food to feed the growing population, many of the Indians would have to be released to return to their traditional encampments. If that happened, the mission and the missionaries would have failed their secular and religious obligations and responsibilities. The paradox was thus created—the proceeds realized from selling certain Indians into slavery would enable the missionaries to save other indigenous souls, perhaps to sell them later to save more Indian souls.

The Jesuits and Franciscans must have consoled themselves by believing the families who received the Apaches promised to feed, clothe, educate, and Christianize their new slaves. Whether they openly admitted it, they knew many of the new owners would not keep this promise; that fact was actually of no consequence. What mattered most of all was continuing their work, so the harsh, unforgivable philosophy of any means to an end ultimately prevailed over moral considerations.

Matson and Fontana conclude, "In the final analysis, the Spanish conquest was more than the coming together of Spanish culture and the cultures of native peoples. It was the establishment of an integrated system of domination . . . [T]here can be no greater form of violence than this."[24] There is no doubt that the imperious agents of the Spanish empire endorsed this inhumanity in the name of the cross and crown.

Also, let us not forget that the holy Bible conferred "dominion" on Christians.[25] It may be said that the priests' actions as representatives of Roman Catholicism reflected their belief that the Bible granted them permission to indoctrinate the indigenes into their faith using whatever methods necessary to guarantee salvation, including genocide.

Their efforts at indoctrination and conversion were successful. Many contemporary members of America's southwestern tribes, the descendants of the survivors, today practice Roman Catholicism. Hanging behind the altar at St. Joseph's Mission on the Mescalero Apache Reservation, where many Chiricahua Apaches live, is a very large oil painting of Christ as an Apache, undeniably and silently honoring the Roman Catholic missionaries who forced their European religion onto the Indians so long ago. As I sit alone in the stillness of that magnificent stone cathedral before Sunday morning mass, I hear the cries of the enslaved ancestors who lost not only their identities and their sacred lands, but their lives as well, all in the name of Christianity.

Chronology

꿎

ca. 1440	Chiricahua Apaches arrive in northern Mexico.
1500–1600	Jesuits arrive in northern Mexico.
1514	Requerimiento is issued, a legal document mandating that the Indians acknowledge the Roman Catholic Church and the pope as ruler of the world and allow the faith to be preached to them.
1520–21	Hernán Cortés arrives in central Mexico.
1533	Slave raids begin on Mexico's west coast.
1542	New Laws seek to abolish the encomienda and prescribe good treatment of Indian slaves and preservation of Indian cultures.
1636	First Jesuit mission established at Ures.
1680–1704	Janos established, destroyed, and reestablished.
1687–1711	Eusebio Kino, SJ, is active in northern Mexico.
1687	Kino first visits San Ignacio.
1690	Kino establishes his headquarters at Magdalena.
1690	Kino first visits San Xavier del Bac.
1690–91	Kino first visits Guévavi and Tumacácori.
1695	Mission buildings at San Ignacio and Tubutama are destroyed in Pima uprising.
1695	Kino celebrates first mass in November at Suamca.
1700	Building begins at San Xavier del Bac, but is soon halted.
1729	Reglamento creates a uniform system of defense in northern borderlands and forbids enslaving Apaches. Captives are to be sent to Mexico City, where viceroy will decide their fate. Some may be imprisoned near presidios and then exchanged for Spanish prisoners.
1746	Suamca becomes a cabecera.
1751	Pima revolt breaks out.
1752–57	Tubac presidio is established.
1756	First baptism takes place at Calabazas.

1756	Construction begins again on San Xavier del Bac.
1767	Jesuits are expelled from northern Mexico.
1767	José Gálvez and the Marqués de Rubí tour northern New Spain.
1768	Fifteen Franciscans arrive in northern Mexico.
1768	Suamca is destroyed and abandoned until 1787.
1768	Cocóspera is destroyed and abandoned until 1787.
1768	San Ignacio becomes a cabecera.
1769	In April, a major Apache attack occurs at San Xavier del Bac.
1770	Tumacácori becomes a cabecera.
1772	Reglamento prohibits abuse of Indian prisoners of war, reinforces dispersion of captives as in 1729 Reglamento, and advocates intensive warfare.
1776	Guévavi is abandoned, and its functions moved to Tumacácori.
1776	Tubac presidio and military personnel are relocated to Tucson.
1779	Royal order requiring humane treatment of all surrendered Indians is issued with no suggestion that they be deported.
1783	Tubac is abandoned.
1786	Instructions are issued containing three main objectives to subdue Apaches: formation of alliances with other tribes against them; continuation of intense warfare against them; and offering peace through surrender and peace establishments. There is no mention of deportation.
1786	Calabazas residents are assimilated into Tumacácori.
1787	Viceroy directs that all Apache captives be shipped to Havana, Cuba.
1787	Large numbers of Apaches begin surrendering at missions.
1799	Deportation of Apaches to Cuba becomes mandatory.

Notes

℀

Notes to Introduction

1. Definitions of frontiers vary widely, but I like the most basic description, for example, "contested ground." Donna J. Guy and Thomas E. Sheridan, "On Frontiers," in *Contested Ground: Comparative Frontiers on the Northern and Southern Edges of the Spanish Empire*, ed. Donna J. Guy and Thomas E. Sheridan (Tucson: University of Arizona Press, 1998), 10.

2. Vine Deloria Jr., *Spirit and Reason: The Vine Deloria Reader* (Golden, CO: Fulcrum publishing, 1999), 86. Deloria eloquently debunks this accepted premise.

3. Richard J. Perry, *Apache Reservation: Indigenous Peoples & the American State* (Austin: University of Texas Press, 1993), 29.

4. Kieran McCarty, OFM, explained the origin of the name. "When a Spanish expedition crossed Arizona in about 1550, they met some native women washing at a stream. The Spaniards spoke to them, asking who they were and they answered 'pianmatt' which means 'I don't understand.' So, the Spanish called them Pimas" and named their destination the Pimería Alta. H. Henrietta Stockel, *On the Bloody Road to Jesus: Christianity and the Chiricahua Apaches* (Albuquerque: University of New Mexico Press, 2004), xvii.

5. Churchill states that Columbus's programs reduced the Taino population from eight million to perhaps a hundred thousand by the time he himself left the islands. The consequences of his policies remained, however, so that by 1542 only two hundred Taino were alive. Ward Churchill, "Confronting Columbus Day," in *Acts of Rebellion: The Ward Churchill Reader*, ed. Ward Churchill (New York: Routledge, 2003), 53.

6. For a detailed description of traditional Chiricahua Apache religious beliefs, see Stockel, *On the Bloody Road to Jesus*, chapter 1.

7. Claire R. Farrer, *Living Life's Circle: Mescalero Apache Cosmovision* (Albuquerque: University of New Mexico Press, 1991), 23.

8. Gen. 1:26–28.

9. John L. Kessell, *Mission of Sorrows: Jesuit Guevavi and the Pimas, 1691–1767* (Tucson: University of Arizona Press, 1970), 59.

10. Clara Sue Kidwell, Homer Noley, and George E. "Tink" Tinker, *A Native American Theology* (Maryknoll, NY: Orbis Books, 2001), 185n13.

Notes to Chapter 1

1. Farrer, *Living Life's Circle*, 18. This reference could have been to two places, either Mongolia or the area around the Arctic Circle. In the late 1800s, Lt. Charles B. Gatewood, one of the U.S. Army officers deeply involved in military campaigns against the Chiricahua Apaches, recorded some of what he had learned from them during his long association. One note was entitled "Origin of the Apaches," and he wrote, "Tradition as coming from the N.W., probably Mongolian-Chinese. Similar words, tunes, medicines." "Origin of the Apaches," 1–4.

2. Farrer, *Living Life's Circle*, 25. This is a difficult book to get through but worth the effort.

3. Julia Cruikshank, "Oral History, Narrative Strategies, and Native American Historiography," in *Clearing a Path: Theorizing the Past in Native American Studies*, ed. Nancy Shoemaker (New York: Routledge, 2002), 10. Wikipedia reports that the territory the Tlingit historically occupied extended from the Portland Canal along the present border between Alaska and British Columbia north to the coast just southeast of the Cooper River delta. The Tlingit occupied almost all the Alexander Archipelago. Through legend the Tlingits claim to have been on the first Mongolian migratory wave across the Bering Strait. http://en.wikipedia.org/wiki/Tlingit. Cruikshank believes the Athapaskans were "adjacent" to the Tlingits, and trade consisted of swapping "perishable . . . coastal marine products for tanned hides and tailored clothing from the interior." "Oral History," 10.

4. Stockel, *On the Bloody Road to Jesus*, xv.

5. Perry, "The Apachean Transition from the Subarctic to the Southwest," *Plains Anthropologist* 25, no. 90 (1980): 279, 281, 293.

6. Kieran McCarty, OFM, interview with author, January 12, 1999.

7. Jack D. Forbes, *Apache, Navaho, and Spaniard* (Norman: University of Oklahoma Press, 1960), xiv–xix.

8. Gary Clayton Anderson, *The Indian Southwest 1580–1830: Ethnogenesis and Reinvention* (Norman: University of Oklahoma Press, 1999), 4. Ethnogenesis and reinvention would become an Apache trait in northern Mexico before contact with Europeans and would hold true during the Spanish occupation.

9. For more information about Chiricahua Apache legends, see Morris

Edward Opler, *Myths and Tales of the Chiricahua Apache Indians* (Lincoln: University of Nebraska Press, 1994).

10. Edwin R. Sweeney, *Cochise: Chiricahua Apache Chief* (Norman: University of Oklahoma Press, 1991), 339.

11. Harry Hoijer, *Chiricahua and Mescalero Apache Texts with Ethnological Notes by Morris E. Opler* (Chicago: University of Chicago Press, 1938), 13.

12. Eve Ball, *In the Days of Victorio: Recollections of a Warm Springs Apache* (Tucson: University of Arizona Press, 1981), 68–70. There are many versions of this tale.

13. Keith H. Basso, *Wisdom Sits in Places: Landscape and Language among the Western Apache* (Albuquerque: University of New Mexico Press, 1996), 38.

14. Kidwell, Noley, and Tinker, *A Native American Theology*, 7, 14, 126–27.

15. David L. Carmichael et al., eds., *Sacred Sites, Sacred Places* (New York: Routledge, 1994), 3.

16. Sweeney, *Cochise*, 339.

17. Eve Ball, *Indeh: An Apache Odyssey* (Provo, UT: Brigham Young University Press, 1980), 56–57.

18. Stockel, *On the Bloody Road to Jesus*, 1.

19. James S. Griffith, *Beliefs and Holy Places: A Spiritual Geography of the Pimería Alta* (Tucson: University of Arizona Press, 1992), xvi. Griffith describes the Pimería Alta as a "varied land. From the eastern oak and grass country westward through the range of mesquites and saguaros to the sparse bushes of the Colorado, the country slopes downhill getting hotter and drier as it does so. Separating ranges are valleys . . . The river valleys are the traditional highways of the eastern Pimeria Alta . . . In present-day terms it stretches from the Gila River on the north to the Mexican International Highway 2 on the south and from the valleys of the San Pedro and Magdalena rivers on the east to a bit west of Ajo."

20. H. Henrietta Stockel, *Women of the Apache Nation: Voices of Truth* (Reno: University of Nevada Press, 1991), 15–16.

21. John G. Bourke, *Apache Medicine Men* (New York: Dover Publications, 1993), 12–13. In addition to being an army officer, Bourke was a noted ethnologist who was also an aide to Gen. George Crook, serving in that capacity until 1883. He took part in many of Crook's Indian operations and wrote about them afterward. His observations are invaluable, including one about the drums used in ceremonies. Bourke wrote, "The drum is nearly always improvised from an iron kettle, partially filled with water and covered with a piece of cloth, well soaped and drawn as tight as possible. The drumstick does not terminate in a ball . . . but is curved into a circle and the stroke is not perpendicular to the surface, but is often given from one side to the other." *Apache Medicine Men*, 12. Additionally, despite this comment that the sounds were "gibberish," they were not,

being vocables, a sequence of sounds rather than a unit of meaning, such as a word. At ceremonies today, the singers still use vocables.

22. Bobette Perrone, H. Henrietta Stockel, and Victoria Krueger, *Medicine Women, Curanderas, and Women Doctors* (Norman: University of Oklahoma Press, 1989), 52–53.

23. Stockel, *On the Bloody Road to Jesus*, 31.

24. Stockel, *On the Bloody Road to Jesus*, 32.

25. Stockel, *On the Bloody Road to Jesus*, 32.

26. Stockel, *Women of the Apache Nation*, 14–15.

27. John G. Bourke, *Medicine Men of the Apache. Ninth Annual Report of the Bureau of Ethnology to the Secretary of the Smithsonian Institution, 1887–88* (Washington, D.C.: U.S. Government Printing Office, 1892), 479–80.

28. Stockel, *Women of the Apache Nation*, 65.

29. One of the curiosities of frontier mission life, where so many indigenes from all tribes died from epidemics of contagious diseases, was the burial practices. Were the non-Christian Indians, many of whom were already on the path to Christianity, buried with Christian sacraments? If the ground could not be effectively opened to place the body deep enough to avoid exhumation by roaming animals, where were they buried? Did public health issues, as we understand it today, ever arise because of the numbers of dead? Did the priest allow the surviving family members to continue the traditional after-death observances?

30. H. Henrietta Stockel, *Survival of the Spirit: Chiricahua Apaches in Captivity* (Reno: University of Nevada Press, 1993), 15.

31. Morris Edward Opler, *An Apache Life-Way: The Economic, Social, & Religious Institutions of the Chiricahua Indians* (Lincoln: University of Nebraska Press, 1996), 229–37.

32. Perry, *Apache Reservation*, 35.

33. Opler, *An Apache Life-way*, 242–48.

34. Stockel, *On the Bloody Road to Jesus*, 38–39.

35. Stockel, *On the Bloody Road to Jesus*, 40.

36. Hoijer and Opler note that the puberty rite is also a social function. During the time the Apaches depended on hunting and gathering, including the Spanish colonial frontier period, "no large section of a tribe could be together for a long period of time. The Girl's Puberty Rite acted as the social occasion. . . . It became the focal point around which the natural desire for tribesmen of a locality to meet, exchange views and property, greet old friends and make new ones, became crystallized. And so the custom arose of expressing thanks and delight that a daughter or close relative had grown to womanhood by playing host and providing food and entertainment for all who cared to come." *Chiricahua and Mescalero Apache Texts*, 104.

37. Stockel, *On the Bloody Road to Jesus*, 275n66.

38. Opler, *Myths and Tales*, 74–75.

39. Opler, *Myths and Tales*, 82–83.
40. Opler, *Myths and Tales*, 79–80.
41. Opler, *Myths and Tales*, 28.
42. David L. Carmichael, "Places of Power," in *Sacred Sites, Sacred Places*, ed. David L. Carmichael et al. (New York: Routledge, 1994), 93.
43. Angie Debo, *Geronimo: The Man, His Time, His Place* (Norman: University of Oklahoma Press, 1976), 8.

Notes to Chapter 2

1. Kieran McCarty, OFM, "Jesuits and Franciscans," in *The Pimeria Alta: Missions and More*, ed. James E. Officer, Mardith Scheutz-Miller, and Bernard L. Fontana (Tucson: The Southwestern Mission Research Center, 1996), 35.
2. Nicholas Bleser, *Tumacacori: From Rancheria to National Monument* (n.p., n.d.), 4, 8.
3. Bleser, *Tumacacori*, 4.
4. Ward Churchill, "The Law Stood Squarely on its Head: U.S. Doctrine, Indigenous Self-Determination, and the Question of World Order," in *Acts of Rebellion: The Ward Churchill Reader*, ed. Ward Churchill (New York: Routledge, 2003), 5.
5. Charles W. Polzer, SJ, *Rules and Precepts of the Jesuit Missions of Northwestern New Spain* (Tucson: University of Arizona Press, 1976), 7.
6. Kessell, *Mission of Sorrows*, 170.
7. Robert Christian Perez, "Indian Rebellions in Northwestern New Spain: A Comparative Analysis, 1695–1750s" (PhD diss., University of California, Riverside, 2003), 231.
8. Charles W. Polzer, SJ, telephone conversation with author, June 10, 2000. Polzer said the military was responsible for the actual punishments that ranged from mild to severe. The priests stood by as the Indian was being disciplined, though.
9. Perez, "Indian Rebellions," 123–24.
10. For information regarding the step-by-step construction of buildings, see Buford Pickens, ed., *The Missions of Northern Sonora: A 1935 Field Documentation* (Tucson: University of Arizona Press, 1993), 8–11.
11. Theodore E. Treutlein, "The Economic Regime of the Jesuit Missions in Eighteenth Century Sonora," *Pacific Historical Review* 8 (1939): 290–91.
12. Robert C. West, *Sonora: Its Geographical Personality* (Austin: University of Texas Press, 1993), 37.
13. West, *Sonora*. 37.
14. Edward H. Spicer, *Cycles of Conquest: The Impact of Spain, Mexico, and the United States on the Southwest, 1533–1960* (Tucson: University of Arizona Press, 1962), 300.
15. Thomas H. Naylor and Charles W. Polzer, SJ, eds., *The Presidio and Militia*

on the *Northern Frontier of New Spain 1570–1700* (Tucson: University of Arizona Press, 1986), 18.

16. Max L. Moorhead, *The Presidio: Bastion of the Spanish Borderlands* (Norman: University of Oklahoma Press, 1975), 5.

17. Dan L. Thrapp described the Pimería Alta as being enormous in extent, stretching from the willow thickets along the Colorado into the broken mountains beyond the Rio Grande and from the great canyons of the north southward for a thousand miles into Mexico. Stockel, *On the Bloody Road to Jesus*, 7.

18. Roberto Mario Salmón, *Indian Revolts in Northern New Spain: A Synthesis of Resistance* (Lanham, MD: University Press of America, 1991), 123.

19. Salmón, *Indian Revolts in Northern New Spain*, 122, 125, 128.

20. A detailed description of the obligations is in Daniel S. Matson and Bernard L. Fontana, eds. and trans., *Father Bringas Reports to the King: Methods of Indoctrination on the Frontier of New Spain 1796–97* (Tucson: University of Arizona Press, 1977), 12.

21. The phrase "Christian [Catholic] evolution" is taken from Robert W. Hefner, "Introduction: World Building and the Rationality of Conversion," in *Conversion to Christianity: Historical and Anthropological Perspectives*, ed. Robert W. Hefner (Berkeley: University of California press, 1993), 6. Briefly, it refers to "greater reasoning ability" and "deeper ethical awareness."

22. Perez, "Indian Rebellions," 237.

23. Donald C. Cutter and Iris Engstrand, *Quest for Empire: Spanish Settlement in the Southwest* (Golden, CO: Fulcrum Publishing, 1996), 120.

24. Segesser, quoted in Kessell, *Mission of Sorrows*, 94.

25. Kessell, *Mission of Sorrows*, 187.

26. Kessell, *Mission of Sorrows*, 52.

27. Perez, "Indian Rebellions," 291–92.

28. The highest ranking position with the Jesuit province of New Spain. He was the administrative head of the entire mission province. In practice, a father visitor, delegated by the provincial, handled each province.

29. Daniel T. Reff, "Critical Introduction," in *History of the Triumphs of our Holy Faith Amongst the Most Barbarous and Fierce Peoples of the New World*, by Andrés Pérez de Ribas, trans. Daniel T. Reff, Maureen Ahearn, and Richard K. Danford, annotated by Daniel T. Reff (Tucson: University of Arizona Press, 1999), 35.

30. David J. Weber, *The Spanish Frontier in North America* (New Haven, CT: Yale University Press, 1992), 15.

31. Charles W. Polzer, SJ, interview with author, January 27, 1999.

32. Oakah L. Jones Jr., *Los Paisanos: Spanish Settlers on the Northern Frontier of New Spain* (Norman: University of Oklahoma Press, 1979), 177.

33. Kidwell, Noley, and Tinker, *A Native American Theology*, 7.

34. Robert H. Jackson, *New Views of Borderlands History* (Albuquerque: University of New Mexico Press, 1998), 4.

35. Lyle W. Williams, "Struggle for Survival: The Hostile Frontier of New Spain, 1750–1800" (PhD diss., Texas Christian University, 1970), 43.

36. David Sweet, "The Ibero-American Frontier Mission in Native American History," in *The New Latin American Mission History*, ed. Eric Langer and Robert H. Jackson (Lincoln: University of Nebraska Press, 1995), 19, 32.

37. Silvio Zavala, "The Frontiers of Hispanic America," in *New Spain's Far Northern Frontier: Essays on Spain in the American West 1540–1821*, ed. David J. Weber (Albuquerque: University of New Mexico Press, 1979), 189–90.

38. Robert H. Jackson, *Indian Population Decline: The Missions of Northwestern New Spain, 1687–1840* (Albuquerque: University of New Mexico Press, 1994), 56–57.

39. Kay Parker Schweinfurth, *Prayer on Top of the Earth: The Spiritual Universe of the Plains Indians* (Boulder: University Press of Colorado, 2002), 193–97.

40. Susan M. Deeds, "Indigenous Responses to Mission Settlement in Nueva Vizcaya," in *Jesuit Encounters in the New World: Jesuit Chroniclers, Geographers, Educators, and Missionaries in the Americas, 1549–1767*, ed. Joseph A. Gagliano and Charles E. Ronan, SJ (Rome: Institutum Historicum S.Il, 1997), 291.

41. Kessell, *Mission of Sorrows*, 92.

42. For an example, see Stockel, *On the Bloody Road to Jesus*, 39–40.

43. Charlotte M. Gradie, "Jesuit Missionaries and Native Elites in Northern Mexico," *Center for Latin American and Caribbean Studies, Occasional Paper 8* (Storrs, CT: Center for Latin American and Caribbean Studies, 1997), 14. Gradie adds that the Jesuits put themselves at risk of native retaliation as a consequence of public punishment.

44. Nicholas Griffiths, introduction to *Spiritual Encounters: Interactions between Christianity and Native Religions in Colonial America*, ed. Nicholas Griffiths and Fernando Cervantes (Birmingham, UK: University of Birmingham Press, 1999), 23.

45. Kidwell, Noley, and Tinker, *A Native American Theology*, 11.

46. Bartolomé Castaños, SJ, founded Nuestra Señora de la Concepción de Baviacora in 1638. Located on the Sonora River, it became a *visita* of Aconchi.

47. Ures was the capital of Sonora for many years and the mission church was the second largest in Sonora.

48. Nicolás de Perera, SJ, to Felipe Segesser, SJ, November 30, 1749. Yale University Jesuit Missionary Collection (hereinafter JMC), WA MSS S-1143, box 2, folder 56.

49. Felipe Segesser, SJ, to Father Gallardo, December 17, 1749. JMC WA MSS S-1143, box 2, folder 60, and box 2, folder 61.

50. Sources are: Officer, Shuetz-Miller, and Fontana, *The Pimeria Alta*; Ignaz Pfefferkorn, *Sonora: A Description of the Province* (Tucson: University of Arizona Press, 1989); Juan Nentvig, SJ, *Rudo Ensayo: A Description of Sonora and Arizona in 1764*, trans. Alberto Francisco Pradeau and Robert R. Rasmussen (Tucson: University of Arizona press, 1980); and Harry J. Karns, *Luz de Tierra Incognita: Juan Mateo Manje; Unknown Arizona and Sonora 1693–1701* (Tucson: Arizona Silhouettes, 1954).

51. Kessell, *Mission of Sorrows*, 92n16.

52. Jake Ivey, "Building Missions," *Bajada: Joining Research and Management* 6, no. 1 (1998): 5. A single dried brick measuring 3 × 13 × 20 inches weighted about forty pounds.

53. Kessell, *Mission of Sorrows*, 79.

54. Kessell, *Mission of Sorrows*, 80.

55. John L. Kessell extensively addresses Guévavi in *Friars, Soldiers, and Reformers: Hispanic Arizona and the Sonora Mission Frontier, 1767–1856* (Tucson: University of Arizona Press, 1976).

56. Bernard Fontana, "Biography of a Desert Church: The Story of Mission San Xavier del Bac," *The Smoke Signal* (Spring 1996): 3.

57. San Xavier del Bac is one of the most beautiful churches in the Southwest. A reclining mannequin of St. Francis lies open, covered with a blanket on which the faithful have pinned hospital wristlets, photos of children and animals, and in January 1999, a photo of an intrauterine ultrasound scan of a developing embryo. A year after the Jesuit expulsion in 1767, Franciscans arrived at Bac and began construction again. Literature about this remarkable edifice is abundant.

58. Officer, Schuetz-Miller, and Fontana, *The Pimeria Alta*, 83.

59. Pickens, *The Missions of Northern Sonora*, 113.

60. Perez, "Indian Rebellions," 213.

61. Officer, Schuetz-Miller, and Fontana, *The Pimeria Alta*, 68.

62. Nentvig, *Rudo Ensayo*, 27, 82. This account is a classic.

63. Charles William Polzer, SJ, "Evolution of the Jesuit Mission System in Northern New Spain, 1600–1767" (PhD diss., University of California, Riverside, 2003), 111.

64. An extensive list of the Sonoran herbs and their applications can be found in the classic work by Nentvig, *Rudo Ensayo*, 43–53.

65. Henry Dobyns, *Tubac Through Four Centuries*, chapter 3, http://dizzy.library.arizona.edu/images/dobyns/cpt3-E.htm. Dobyns described the earliest epidemics, mainly smallpox, as occurring in 1607, 1641, 1646, 1662, 1740, and 1724. Measles struck in 1728–29. Between 1732 and 1751, at least five epidemics occurred at Guévavi, and four of those five reoccurred every other year between 1744 and 1751. Typhus struck Magdalena in 1737, and smallpox decimated San Ignacio that same year. Between 1749 and 1751, deadly contagion swept the missions of San Ignacio, Guévavi, Sonoitac, and

Magdalena again and again. The crude mortality rate at Guévavi has been estimated to be 152.2 deaths per 1000 during 1766. The electronic version of *Tubac Through Four Centuries*, used exclusively in this book, is located at arizona.edu/tubac/about.htm. The Arizona State Parks Board prepared the original edition during creation of the Tubac Presidio Historical State Park. The board commissioned the Arizona State Museum to organize and summarize all available historical material concerning Tubac Presidio from its creation until it ceased to exist as a military fort. Henry Dobyns undertook this project as a 1959 report. The contents of this web version was created from a version reformatted by the Tubac Presidio Historical State Park in August 1995. During the summer of 1997 the Word files were converted to HTML. Few changes have been made to the format. Mostly, the chapters were arbitrarily divided into smaller files to facilitate readers' access.

66. Polzer, "Evolution of the Jesuit Mission System," 94–95.

67. Polzer, "Evolution of the Jesuit Mission System," 96.

68. Clara Sue Kidwell, *Choctaws and Missionaries in Mississippi, 1818–1918* (Norman: University of Oklahoma Press, 1995), 85.

69. Taken from a sign in an exhibit at San Xavier del Bac's museum. The reasons for the Jesuit expulsion have never been precisely identified.

70. Charles W. Polzer, SJ, interview with author, January 27, 1999.

71. Joseph Och, SJ., *Missionary in Sonora: The Travel Reports of Joseph Och, S.J., 1755–1767*, trans. Theodore Treutlein (San Francisco: California Historical Society, 1965), 55–56.

72. About a hundred miles north of Mexico City.

73. Louis Caywood, "The Spanish Missions of Northwestern New Spain: Franciscan Period, 1768–1836," *The Kiva* 6, no. 4 (1941): 14.

74. Most Rev. J. B. Salpointe, DD, *Soldiers of the Cross: Notes on the Ecclesiastical History of New Mexico, Arizona, and Colorado* (Banning, CA: St. Boniface's Industrial School, 1898), 140.

75. Charles R. Carlisle and Bernard L. Fontana, "Sonora in 1773: Reports by Five Jaliscan Friars (Part 1)." *Arizona and the West* (Spring 1969): 45. An important difference between a mission and a parish is that individuals comprising a mission are not yet full Christians, as are the people comprising a parish.

76. Kessell, *Friars, Soldiers, and Reformers*, 23, 42.

77. Kessell, *Friars, Soldiers, and Reformers*, 43.

78. This information is a summary of Kessell, *Friars, Soldiers, and Reformers*, 17–18.

79. Salpointe, *Soldiers of the Cross*, 140.

80. Kessell, *Friars, Soldiers, and Reformers*, 42.

81. Donald T. Garate, *Los Santos Ángeles de Guevavi* (Tucson, AZ: Southwest Parks and Monuments Association, 2000), 7.

82. Donald T. Garate, *San Cayetano de Calabazas* (Tucson, AZ: Southwest Parks and Monuments Association, 2000), 3.

83. Kieran McCarty, OFM, *Desert Documentary: The Spanish Years, 1767–1821* (Tucson: Arizona Historical Society, 1976), 9.

84. As this is being written, attempts are under way to excavate the wall, now in the center of Tucson.

85. Pickens, *The Missions of Northern Sonora*, 34.

86. Fontana, *Biography of a Desert Church*, 20.

87. Zephyrin Englehardt, OFM, *Franciscans in Arizona* (Harbor Springs, MI: n.p., 1899), 39.

88. Alfred F. Whiting, ed. "The Tumacacori Census of 1796," *The Kiva* 19 (1953): 2–3. One important concept must not be overlooked: putative fatherhood. While very little research has been done into this area, it is possible that some priests themselves—Jesuits and Franciscans—were the biological fathers of some of these children and gave their sons their own names.

89. Kessell, *Mission of Sorrows*, 60.

90. Kessell, *Friars, Soldiers, and Reformers*, 246.

91. Englehardt, *The Franciscans in Arizona*, 170.

92. Caywood, "The Spanish Missions of Northwestern New Spain," 15.

93. Inga Clendinnen, *Ambivalent Conquests: Maya and Spaniard in Yucatan, 1517–1570* (London: Cambridge University Press, 1987), 46–49.

94. Weber, *The Spanish Frontier in North America*, 229.

95. Kieran McCarty, OFM, interviews with author at San Xavier del Bac mission, January 5 and January 12, 1999.

Notes to Chapter 3

1. Perez, "Indian Rebellions," 309. It is no secret the priests were also ill from other than chronic diseases. Ailments such as uncontrolled anger, alcoholism, and sexually transmitted diseases were also part of the human landscape and did not discriminate between priest and indigene. Keller may have been drinking when he embarrassed Luis.

2. Two priests, one hundred Spaniards, and an unknown number of peaceful Indians were killed. Churches were burned and holy objects profaned. Literature about the Pima Revolt is abundant.

3. Tubac today is an artists' colony with a growing area of upscale developments nearby.

4. On March 18, 1752, long after the main revolt ended, Luis the instigator surrendered at Tubac, claiming the devil made him do it. Either he had been exposed to Christianity and believed what he was saying, hoping the Roman Catholic Spaniards would excuse his actions, or the Jesuits interpreted his words to include the reference as they understood it. In any case it was clever of him, and he was not killed on the spot.

5. Dobyns names these as the new governor, Juan Antonio Tuburuca, his wife Inés, and their son Andrés; the new captain, Phelipe Bicani, his wife Rosa, and their son Isidro; the new *mador* (teacher of religious doctrine), Hernando Jurana, and his wife Rosa-María. The other Pimas, those with no official titles were Bartholo and his wife Catharine; Cristóval and his wife Rosa; a single man named Sivibuta; Francisco and his wife Margarita; Francisco Tivtuburi and his wife Juana; Juan and his wife Xaviera; Miguel Tovpon, his wife Ynés, and their two unidentified sons, ages six and eight; Joseph Ignacio, his wife Nicolasa, and their unidentified son, age six; Juan Antonio and his wife Anna María; nine bachelors; and four widows. These names are important in that these residents could have received Apache captives as slaves, and the slaves would have been baptized with their owners' names, making it possible but not probable that the families could still be traced today.

6. Dobyns, *Tubac Through Four Centuries*, chapter 6. Tumacácori was then a visita of Guévavi, but Dobyns postulates that a continuing influx of new residents could have convinced the Franciscans, later in the 1770s, to transfer Guévavi's status as a cabecera to Tumacácori. This conclusion is incorrect.

7. The Sobaípuris are closely related to the Pimas.

8. Fay Jackson Smith, John L. Kessell, and Francis J. Fox, SJ, have written *Father Kino in Arizona* (Phoenix: Arizona Historical Foundation, 1966), an incredible book that includes Kino's diary describing his 1691 travels among the missions. Almost without exception, he notes that the Indians welcomed him with lines of people waiting to see him, flowers, arches, and food. All along the route the indigenes offered him their infants and children to baptize.

9. Smith, Kessell, and Fox, *Father Kino in Arizona*, 69–71.

10. Dobyns states that Beldarrain, like other Spaniards on the frontier, enriched himself and his family through his position. He acquired Apache slaves, arranged advantageous marriages for his children, and named Anza as godfather for his son but also suffered heartaches during his tenure with the deaths of two of his young children, a son and daughter. Dobyns, *Tubac Through Four Centuries*, chapter 6. Beldarrain was buried beneath the steps leading to Guévavi's altar.

11. Dobyns, *Tubac Through Four Centuries*, chapter 6. Some of the campaigns are: June 2, 1752—Thirty men rode out from Tubac to the east to fight Apaches; February and March 1766—Anza with a combined force from several posts and Pima scouts rode east, took forty captives, and distributed them by lot among the troops. Rode on to San Simon, killed two Apaches, and took forty more captives; December 1768—With Anza in California, his lieutenant took twenty-six soldiers and fifty Indian auxiliaries on a scout looking for Apaches. Found too many and retreated but not until the soldiers killed two Apaches and wounded others; April 3, 1769—Apaches attacked eight

Indians guarding San Xavier del Bac. Ten soldiers from Tubac, fifteen citizens, and forty Pimas followed the troops but retreated because of too many Apaches; March 1770—Anza and sixty troops out on a scout; July-August 1771—Anza, thirty-four soldiers, and fifty Pimas killed nine Apaches, took eight prisoners, and recovered one Spanish captive; 1772—Offensive against Apaches continued by setting up an advance post at San Bernadino. Was a joint enterprise between two forts—Tubac and Terrannte; 1773—Early in the year Anza was at San Bernadino and with an officer scouted, found eleven Apaches at San Simón, and took three prisoners.

12. Maria Soledad Arbelaez, "The Sonoran Missions and Indian Raids of the Eighteenth Century," *Journal of the Southwest* 33, no. 3 (1991): 368.

13. McCarty, *Desert Documentary*, 73–74, 78.

14. Dobyns, *Tubac Through Four Centuries*, chapter 6. Anza believed in using Indian auxiliaries to fight Apaches or Seris. In that regard, he made every effort to employ Pimas. A little more than a century later, Gen. George Crook adopted the same strategy and used Chiricahua, San Carlos, and White Mountain Apaches to fight the Chiricahuas on American soil. Anza was descended from a long line of military men, including his father, whom Apaches killed in an ambush in 1739, two years after he nearly beat to death Augustín Aschuhul, a Guaymas native he suspected of causing trouble. After the man confessed, the elder Anza shot him to death. Perez, "Indian Rebellions," 254–56. The younger Anza was born in Fronteras, Mexico, in 1735 and took charge of Tubac at the age of twenty-five.

15. Dobyns, *Tubac Through Four Centuries*, chapter 6. This extralegal system operated on the same assumptions Spanish troops had used to rid Spain of the Moors. War captives were treated as slaves who could be retained and put to forced labor or sold for cash.

16. Zavala, "The Frontiers of Hispanic America," 187.

17. William B. Griffen, *Apaches at War and Peace: The Janos Presidio, 1750–1858* (Tucson: University of Arizona Press, 1979), 110. These records are dated from 1799 until 1802 and do not specifically state that the owners of these Apache slaves were soldiers. Nonetheless, the information is substantive.

18. Dobyns, *Tubac Through Four Centuries*, chapter 6.

19. Dobyns, *Tubac Through Four Centuries*, chapter 6.

20. Dobyns, *Tubac Through Four Centuries*, chapter 6.

21. Dobyns, *Tubac Through Four Centuries*, chapter 6.

22. John L. Kessell, "Friars versus Bureaucrats: The Mission as a Threatened Institution on the Arizona-Sonora Frontier, 1767–1842," *Western Historical Quarterly* (April 1974): 151. See also Elizabeth A. H. John, *Storms Brewed in Other Men's Worlds: The Confrontation of Indians, Spanish, and French in the Southwest, 1540–1795* (Lincoln: University of Nebraska Press, 1975), 440, where she stated that Anza "saw no hope of true pacification of the Apaches."

23. John, *Storms Brewed in Other Men's Worlds*, 78.

24. Kessell, *Friars, Soldiers, and Reformers*, 133.

25. http://www.nps.gov/tuma/mission 2000.

26. http://www.nps.gov/tuma/mission 2000.

27. http://www.nps.gov/tuma/mission 2000.

28. http://www.nps.gov/tuma/mission 2000.

29. http://www.nps.gov/tuma/mission 2000.

30. http://www.nps.gov/tuma/mission 2000. Either Gil de Bernabé was writing retrospectively, or the date of this entry—three years after Jesuit removal—is incorrect.

31. http://www.nps.gov/tuma/mission 2000.

32. http://www.nps.gov/tuma/mission 2000.

33. http://www.nps.gov/tuma/mission 2000.

34. http://www.nps.gov/tuma/mission 2000.

35. http://data2.itc.nps.gov/tuma/Results.cfm at Mission 2000.

36. http://www.nps.gov/tuma/mission 2000.

37. Peter Alan Stern, "Social Marginality and Acculturation on the Northern Frontier of New Spain" (PhD diss., University of California, Berkeley, 1984), 339–420. Stern devoted an entire chapter of his dissertation to the treatment and fate of captives the Apaches held. He stated that children were great because they could be converted to Apache ways and transformed into Indians more easily than could adults. "In many cases, children captured while young married within the tribe and could not or would not return to their homes and parent cultures" (341).

38. Stockel, *Women of the Apache Nation*, 89.

39. Dobyns, *Tubac Through Four Centuries*, chapter 6.

40. Ana Maria Alonso, *Thread of Blood: Colonialism, Revolution, and Gender on Mexico's Northern Frontier* (Tucson: University of Arizona Press, 1995), 43.

41. Max L. Moorhead, "Spanish Deportation of Hostile Apaches: The Policy and the Practice," *Arizona and the West* 17, no. 3 (1975): 205.

42. Alonso, *Thread of Blood*, 37.

43. Forbes, *Apache, Navajo and Spaniard*, 7.

44. Perez, "Indian Rebellions," 119.

45. The Tumacácori mission was designated a nine-acre national monument in 1908. It was expanded in 1990 to its current forty-six acres, when the mission ruins at Guévavi and Calabazas were added to the park and the 101st Congress designated it a National Historical Park.

46. Cutter and Engstrand, *Quest for Empire*, 160–61.

47. Anza is well known for his background and abilities. Strong and hardy, he seemed extremely capable of enduring the rigors of military life on the colonial frontier. Anza was a firm believer in using Indian auxiliaries, particularly the Pimas, in fighting Apaches.

48. Jones, *Los Paisanos*, 192.

49. Dobyns, *Tubac Through Four Centuries*, chapter 6.

50. Mark Santiago, *The Red Captain: The Life of Hugo O'Conor Commandant Inspector of the Interior Provinces of New Spain*, Museum Monograph 9 (Tucson: Arizona Historical Society, 1994), 35.

51. Ball, *Indeh*, 213.

52. Perez, "Indian Rebellions," 88. There is no information regarding any indigenous group on the frontier between the years 1650 and 1800 conducting this same reverse baptism. The name Perico, however, seems to have been popular. One of Geronimo's warriors, much later in history, was similarly called.

53. Dobyns, *Tubac Through Four Centuries*, chapter 1.

54. Kessell, *Mission of Sorrows*, 39.

55. Kessell, *Mission of Sorrows*, 73–74.

56. Perez, "Indian Rebellions," 118–19.

57. Dobyns, *Tubac Through Four Centuries*, chapter 2.

58. Dobyns, *Tubac Through Four Centuries*, chapter 2.

59. Dobyns, *Tubac Through Four Centuries*, chapter 2.

60. Dobyns goes into detail about these classes and castes in *Tubac Through Four Centuries*, chapter 6.

61. Dobyns, *Tubac Through Four Centuries*, chapter 6.

62. Readers must be warned that the reliability of numbers may be suspect.

63. Dobyns, *Tubac Through Four Centuries*, chapter 6.

64. Dobyns, *Tubac Through Four Centuries*, chapter 6.

65. Kessell, *Mission of Sorrows*, 132.

66. Joseph F. Park, "Spanish Indian Policy in Northern Mexico, 1765–1810," *Plains Anthropologist* 25, no. 90 (1980): 326.

67. Park, "Spanish Indian Policy," 330.

68. Sidney B. Brinckerhoff and Odie B. Faulk, *Lancers for the King: A Study of the Frontier Military System of Northern New Spain with a Translation of the Royal Regulations of 1772* (Phoenix: Arizona Historical Society, 1962), 32–33.

69. Max L. Moorhead, *The Apache Frontier: Jacobo Ugarte and Spanish-Indian Relations in Northern New Spain, 1769–1791* (Norman: University of Oklahoma Press, 1968), 117–18.

70. Moorhead, *The Apache Frontier*, 103.

71. Moorhead, *The Apache Frontier*, 107.

72. Susan Lamb, *Tumacacori: National Historical Park* (Tucson, AZ: Southwest Parks and Monument Association, 1993), 10. Each indigenous group had a unique way of crafting its arrows, unlike any other, so it was easy to identify the raiders.

73. Bleser, *Tumacacori*, 1.

74. Bleser, *Tumacacori*, 11.

75. Perez, "Indian Rebellions," 222.

76. Kessell, *Friars, Soldiers, and Reformers*, 38.

77. The adobe church with a flat roof measured sixty by twenty feet. The east end contained a cemetery, and the sacristy and other rooms were at the south side. Only the restored foundation exists today.

78. Kessell, *Mission of Sorrows*, 157.

79. Kessell, *Mission of Sorrows*, 160.

80. Kessell, *Mission of Sorrows*, 165–66.

81. Apache raiders totally leveled Sonoita in 1768; more than half the population died within its burning walls. McCarty, *Desert Documentary*, 74. The exact location of this mission has not been found. Several sites offer possibilities, however, including one near the Nature Conservancy's building in Patagonia, Arizona. Nothing remains except very low melting adobe walls and the vague outline of a road. People claim to have found broken pieces of pottery, but I found only the walls to indicate habitation.

82. Bleser, *Tumacacori*, 46. Readers must be reminded that dates are arguable.

83. Kessell, *Friars, Soldiers, and Reformers*, 68. Kessell named those who would serve at Tumacácori over an eight-year period: Francisco Sánchez Zúñiga, Bartolomé Ximeno, Gaspar de Clemente, Joseph Matías Moreno, Tomás Eixarch, Juan Bautista Velderrain, Joaquín Antonio Belarde, and Baltazar Carillo. *Friars, Soldiers, and Reformers*, 68n5.

84. In March 1772 Seris murdered Gil de Bernabé, who thus became Sonora's first Franciscan martyr.

85. Christopher Vecsey, *On the Padres' Trail* (Notre Dame, IN: University of Notre Dame Press, 1996), 93.

86. Kessell, *Friars, Soldiers, and Reformers*, 78, 80.

87. Moreno was martyred eight years later by Yuma Indians, far from Tumacácori.

88. Kessell, *Friars, Soldiers, and Reformers*, 101.

89. Kessell, *Friars, Soldiers, and Reformers*, 196.

90. Jesús F. de la Teja and Ross Frank, eds. *Choice, Persuasion, and Coercion: Social Control on Spain's North American Frontiers* (Albuquerque: University of New Mexico Press, 2005), 111. See also Ramón A. Gutiérrez, *When Jesus Came, the Corn Mothers Went Away: Marriage, Sexuality, and Power in New Mexico, 1500–1846* (Stanford, CA: Stanford University Press, 1991), 314.

91. Kessell goes into detail about Gutierrez's moods, machinations, and excuses in *Friars, Soldiers, and Reformers*, 187–90.

92. About seventy-five miles south of Columbus, New Mexico, today.

93. It is possible that the remaining members of these two tribes were later absorbed by the Chiricahua Apaches.

94. Griffen, *Apaches at War and Peace*, 24–27.
95. Records of Janos, Mexican Archives at the Benson Latin American Collection, University of Texas, Austin.
96. Thanks to Matt Babcock and his research at University of Texas, Austin, for this information.
97. Christon I. Archer, "The Deportation of Barbarian Indians from the Internal Provinces of New Spain, 1789–1810," *The Americas* (January 1973): 379.
98. Moorhead, "Spanish Deportation of Hostile Apaches," 214–15.
99. Moorhead, "Spanish Deportation of Hostile Apaches," 212.
100. Archer, "The Deportation of Barbarian Indians," 377.
101. Archer, "The Deportation of Barbarian Indians," 382. Someruelos remained adamantly against his country receiving Apache or any other group of slaves. His complaints fell on deaf ears.

Notes to Chapter 4

1. Moorhead, *The Apache Frontier*, 134.
2. Moorhead, "Spanish Deportation of Hostile Apaches," 213.
3. John, *Storms Brewed in Other Men's Worlds*, 63.
4. Thomas D. Hall, *Social Change in the Southwest, 1350–1880* (Lawrence: University Press of Kansas, 1989), 50, 114.
5. Charles Gibson, *Spain in America* (New York: Harper Torchbooks, 1966), 51.
6. José Cuello, "The Persistence of Indian Slavery and Encomienda in the Northeast of Colonial Mexico, 1577–1723," *Journal of Social History* 21 (Summer 1988): 688.
7. Gibson, *Spain in America*, 51.
8. Cutter and Engstrand, *Quest for Empire*, 114.
9. Gibson, *Spain in America*, 52.
10. Gibson, *Spain in America*, 57n16. Here, Gibson is quoting Motolinía, a sixteenth-century writer.
11. Weber, *The Spanish Frontier in North America*, 126. Repartimiento was abolished in 1632 and replaced by wage labor or debt peonage.
12. Charles Polzer, SJ, "Kino in Mexico" (lecture at Sierra Lutheran Church, Sierra Vista, AZ, February 14, 2001).
13. Lesley Byrd Simpson, *The Encomienda in New Spain: The Beginning of Spanish Mexico* (Berkeley: University of California Press, 1950), 68–70. The role of town councils on the frontier is a study in itself of competing interests for status and forced Indian labor.
14. Robert Ryal Miller and William J. Orr, eds., *Daily Life in Colonial Mexico: The Journey of Friar Ilarione de Bergama, 1761–1768*, trans. William J. Orr (Norman: University of Oklahoma Press, 2000), 65. In addition to private

owners branding their slaves, the authors report that "from the earliest days of Spanish colonization in Puerto Rico, it was the custom when slaves first arrived to give them the brand of the government . . . This was done to discourage smuggling. Thus slaves found working on plantations without the brand were immediately confiscated by the government." Miller and Orr, *Daily Life in Colonial Mexico*, 203.

15. Cuello, "The Persistence of Indian Slavery," 692.

16. Simpson, *The Encomienda in New Spain*, 129–30.

17. Simpson, *The Encomienda in New Spain*, 130–31. Controversy erupted immediately, and through time the New Laws were modified and the provisions tamed. Since the reactions to the New Laws were quite complex and intense, for more information, I suggest reading the Simpson book. Cuello stated that "historians have generally concluded that encomienda was not feasible among hunter-gatherers who were enslaved, incorporated into Hispanic society, wiped out, or who adopted a permanent mode of guerilla warfare." Cuello, "The Persistence of Indian Slavery," 695. It sounds like he was talking about the Apaches.

18. Sheridan, "Social Control and Native Territoriality," in *Choice, Persuasion, and Coercion: Social Control on Spain's North American Frontiers*, ed. Jesús F. de la Teja and Ross Frank (Albuquerque: University of New Mexico Press, 2005), 146.

19. Moorhead, "Spanish Deportation of Hostile Apaches," 205.

20. Jacobo Ugarte y Loyola, Antonio Denojeant, and Henrique de Grimarest, DRSW Master Bibliography, #041–04318; Jacobo Ugarte y Loyola and Francisco Tovar, DRSW Master Bibliography, #041–04319; and Jacobo Ugarte y Loyola, Henrique de Grimarest, and Antonio Denojeant, DRSW Master Bibliography, #041–04321, Arizona State Museum, Documentary Relations of the Southwest Collection (DRSW), University of Arizona, Tucson, Arizona.

21. Stockel, *On the Bloody Road to Jesus*, 94; and Matson and Fontana, *Friar Bringas Reports to the King*, 67.

22. For a biography of Bringas, see Matson and Fontana, *Friar Bringas Reports to the King*, 2–3.

23. Matson and Fontana, *Friar Bringas Reports to the King*, 89.

24. James Officer, *Hispanic Arizona, 1536–1856* (Tucson: University of Arizona Press, 1987), 76.

25. Kessell, *Mission of Sorrows*, 59.

26. Gutiérrez, *When Jesus Came, the Corn Mothers Went Away*, 182.

27. http://www.nps.gov/tuma.

28. Matson and Fontana, *Friar Bringas Reports to the King*, 74.

1. Deni J. Seymour, "The Implications of Mobility, Reoccupation, and Low Visibility Phenomena for Chronometric Dating" (unpublished paper, 2006–7), 32.
2. James F. Brooks, "Life Proceeds from the Name: Indigenous Peoples and the Predicament of Hybridity," in *Clearing a Path: Theorizing the Past in Native American Studies*, ed. Nancy Shoemaker (New York: Routledge, 2002), 190. Brooks cites successful examples of crossover Indians becoming an integral part of their "host" societies.
3. James Axtell, "Some Thoughts on the Ethnohistory of Missions," *Ethnohistory* 29, no. 1 (1982): 39.
4. Kessell, *Mission of Sorrows*, 92.
5. Perez, "Indian Rebellions," 213.
6. Griffen, *Apaches at War and Peace*, 65n11, 110.
7. For a full understanding of the meaning of names to the Western Apaches, see Basso, *Wisdom Sits in Places*.
8. H. Henrietta Stockel, *Chiricahua Apache Women and Children: Safekeepers of the Heritage* (College Station: Texas A & M University Press, 2000), 20–21.
9. Opler, *An Apache Life-way*, 429–31.
10. Stockel, *On the Bloody Road to Jesus*, 34.
11. Reff, "Critical Introduction," 35.
12. William B. Griffen, *Indian Assimilation in the Franciscan Era*, Anthropological Papers of the University of Arizona 33 (Tucson: University of Arizona Press, 1979), 55.
13. Griffen, *Indian Assimilation in the Franciscan Era*, 58.
14. Griffen, *Indian Assimilation in the Franciscan Era*, 23.
15. Stern, "Social Marginality," 109–10. Stern identifies marginals as people who coexist in both societies, are agents of acculturation and transmit knowledge from one society to another, and are the link between two societies on a frontier.
16. Archer, "The Deportation of Barbarian Indians," 381–82. "In Cuba the Indians refused alliance with the African slaves and sought to deal equally and violently with all classes of the population. In one of these incidents, several Apaches escaped custody and embarked on a furious escapade of violence which resulted in the robbery of livestock and the murder of a Negro slave" (383).
17. Moorhead, "Spanish Deportation of Hostile Apaches," 206.
18. Archer, "The Deportation of Barbarian Indians," 377.
19. Moorhead, "Spanish Deportation of Hostile Apaches," 209–10.
20. Moorhead, "Spanish Deportation of Hostile Apaches," 219.
21. Archer, "The Deportation of Barbarian Indians," 381.
22. Churchill, "Confronting Columbus Day," 44.

23. Matson and Fontana, *Father Bringas Reports to the King*, 75.
24. Matson and Fontana, *Father Bringas Reports to the King*, 31.
25. Other biblical permissions are Matthew 28:19–20, "Go ye therefore and teach all nations, baptizing them in the name of the Father, and of the Son, and of the Holy Ghost, teaching them to observe all things whatsoever I have commanded you," and Acts 1:8, "But ye shall receive power, after that the Holy Ghost is come upon you: and ye shall be witnesses unto me both in Jerusalem, and in all Judaea, and in Samaria, and unto the uttermost part of the earth."

Bibliography
℘

Primary Sources

Manuscript Collections

Documentary Relations of the Southwest Collection. Arizona State Museum. University of Arizona, Tucson, Arizona.

Gatewood, Charles B. "Origin of the Apaches." MS 282, box 4, folder 61, Arizona Historical Society, Tucson, Arizona.

Jesuit Missionary Collection. Beinecke Library. Yale University.

Mexican Archives at the Benson Latin American Collection. University of Texas, Austin.

Other Works

Alonso, Ana Maria. *Thread of Blood: Colonialism, Revolution, and Gender on Mexico's Northern Frontier*. Tucson: University of Arizona Press, 1995.

Anderson, Gary Clayton. *The Indian Southwest 1580–1830: Ethnogenesis and Reinvention*. Norman: University of Oklahoma Press, 1999.

Arbelaez, Maria Soledad. "The Sonoran Missions and Indian Raids of the Eighteenth Century." *Journal of the Southwest* 33, no. 3 (1991): 366–85.

Archer, Christon I. "The Deportation of Barbarian Indians from the Internal Provinces of New Spain, 1789–1810." *The Americas* (January 1973): 376–85.

Axtell, James. "Some Thoughts on the Ethnohistory of the Missions." *Ethnohistory* 29, no. 1 (1982): 35–41.

Ball, Eve. *Indeh: An Apache Odyssey*. Provo, UT: Brigham Young University Press, 1980.

———. *In the Days of Victorio: Recollections of a Warm Springs Apache*. Tucson: University of Arizona Press, 1981.

Banks, Leo W. "Legends of the Lost: The Buried Treasure of Mission Guevavi

May Have Been Found and Lost Again." *Arizona Highways* (October 1995): 46–47.

Basso, Keith H. *Wisdom Sits in Places: Landscape and Language among the Western Apache.* Albuquerque: University of New Mexico Press, 1996.

Bleser, Nicholas. *Tumacacori: From Ranchería to National Monument.* N.p., n.d.

Bolton, Herbert. "The Black Robes of New Spain." *Catholic Historical Review* 21 (1935): 257–82.

———. "The Jesuits in America: An Opportunity for Historians." *Mid-America* 18, no. 4 (1936): 223–24.

Bourke, John G. *Apache Medicine Men.* New York: Dover Publications, 1993. (An unabridged replication of an accompanying paper, "The Medicine Men of the Apache," originally 443–603 in the *Ninth Annual Report of the Bureau of Ethnology to the Secretary of the Smithsonian Institution, 1887–88,* as first published in 1892 by the U.S. Government Printing Office, Washington, D.C.)

———. *Medicine Men of the Apache. Ninth Annual Report of the Bureau of Ethnology to the Secretary of the Smithsonian Institution, 1887–88.* Washington, D.C.: U.S. Government Printing Office, 1892.

———. "Notes on Apache Mythology." *Journal of the American Folklore Society* 3 (April–June 1890): 209–12.

Brinckerhoff, Sidney B., and Odie B. Faulk. *Lancers for the King: A Study of the Frontier Military System of Northern New Spain with a Translation of the Royal Regulations of 1772.* Phoenix: Arizona Historical Society, 1962.

Brooks, James F. *Captives & Cousins: Slavery, Kinship, and Community in the Southwest Borderlands.* Chapel Hill: University of North Carolina Press, 2002.

———. "Life Proceeds from the Name: Indigenous Peoples and the Predicament of Hybridity." In *Clearing a Path: Theorizing the Past in Native American Studies,* edited by Nancy Shoemaker, 181–205. New York: Routledge, 2002.

Carlisle, Charles R., and Bernard L. Fontana. "Sonora in 1773: Reports by Five Jaliscan Friars (Part 1)." *Arizona and the West* (Spring 1969): 39–56.

Carmichael, David L. "Places of Power." In *Sacred Sites, Sacred Places,* edited by David L. Carmichael, Jane Hubert, Brian Reeves, and Audhild Schanche. New York: Routledge, 1994.

———, Jane Hubert, Brian Reeves, and Audhild Schanche, eds. *Sacred Sites, Sacred Places.* New York: Routledge, 1994.

Caywood, Louis. "The Spanish Mission of New Spain: Franciscan Period, 1768–1836." *The Kiva* 6, no. 4 (1941): 13–16.

Churchill, Ward. "Confronting Columbus Day." In *Acts of Rebellion: The Ward Churchill Reader,* edited by Ward Churchill, 43–61. New York: Routledge, 2003.

———. "The Law Stood Squarely on its Head: U.S. Doctrine, Indigenous Self-Determination, and the Question of World Order." In *Acts of Rebellion: The Ward Churchill Reader*, edited by Ward Churchill, 3–22. New York, Routledge, 2003.

Clendinnen, Inga. *Ambivalent Conquests: Maya and Spaniard in Yucatan, 1517–1570*. London: Cambridge University Press, 1987.

Cortés, José. *Views from the Apache Frontier: Report on the Northern Provinces of New Spain*. Edited by Elizabeth A. H. John. Translated by John Wheat. Norman: University of Oklahoma Press, 1989.

Cruikshank, Julia. "Oral History, Narrative Strategies, and Native American Historiography." In *Clearing a Path: Theorizing the Past in Native American Studies*, edited by Nancy Shoemaker, 1–27. New York: Routledge, 2002.

Cuello, José. "The Persistence of Indian Slavery and Encomienda in the Northeast of Colonial Mexico, 1577–1723." *Journal of Social History* 21 (Summer 1988): 683–700.

Cutter, Donald C., and Iris Engstrand. *Quest for Empire: Spanish Settlement in the Southwest*. Golden, CO: Fulcrum Publishing, 1996.

Damon, Meffie, Ruby Edwards, Judy Eichman, Don Garate, Maxine Hamilton, Betty Hummer, Rocky Kloster, Ann Rasor, Roy Simpson, Ginny Sphar, and David Yubeta. *In the Footprints of the Past: An Interpretive and Informational Guide to Tumacacori Historical Park*. Tucson, AZ: Southwest Parks and Monuments Association, 1998.

Debo, Angie. *Geronimo: The Man, His Time, His Place*. Norman: University of Oklahoma Press, 1976.

Deeds, Susan M. "Indigenous Responses to Mission Settlement in Nueva Vizcaya." In *Jesuit Encounters in the New World: Jesuit Chroniclers, Geographers, Educators, and Missionaries in the Americas, 1549–1767*, edited by Joseph A. Gagliano and Charles E. Ronan, SJ, 280–304. Rome: Institutum Historicum S.Il, 1997. Also in *The New Latin American Mission History*, edited by Eric Langer and Robert H. Jackson, 77–108. Lincoln: University of Nebraska Press, 1995.

———. *Defiance and Deference in Mexico's Colonial North: Indians under Spanish Rule in Nueva Vizcaya*. Austin: University of Texas Press, 2003.

Deloria, Vine, Jr. *Spirit and Reason: The Vine Deloria, Jr., Reader*. Golden, CO: Fulcrum Publishing, 1999.

Dobyns, Henry. *Tubac Through Four Centuries*. http://dizzy.library.arizona.edu/images/dobyns/cpt3-E.htm.

http://en.wikipedia.org/wiki/Tlingit.

http://www.nps.gov/tuma.

Eckhart, George B. "A Guide to the History of the Missions of Sonora, 1614–1926." *Arizona and the West* 2 (1960): 165–83.

Englehardt, Zephyrin, OFM. *Franciscans in Arizona*. Harbor Springs, MI: n.p., 1899.

Farrer, Claire R. *Living Life's Circle: Mescalero Apache Cosmovision*. Albuquerque: University of New Mexico Press, 1991.

Fontana, Bernard. "Biography of a Desert Church: The Story of Mission San Xavier del Bac." *The Smoke Signal* (Spring 1996): 1–68.

Forbes, Jack D. *Apache, Navaho, and Spaniard*. Norman: University of Oklahoma Press, 1960.

Garate, Donald T. *San Cayetano de Calabazas*. Tucson, AZ: Southwest Parks and Monuments Association, 2000.

———. *Los Santos Ángeles de Guevavi*. Tucson, AZ: Southwest Parks and Monuments Association, 2000.

Giago, Tim. "Spirituality Comes from the Heart, Not from a Book." *American Indian Religions: An Interdisciplinary Journal* 1, no. 1 (1994): 97–98.

Gibson, Charles. *Spain in America*. New York: Harper Torchbooks, 1966.

Gradie, Charlotte M. "Jesuit Missionaries and Native Elites in Northern Mexico, 1572 to 1616." *Center for Latin American and Caribbean Studies, Occasional Paper 8*. Storrs, CT: Center for Latin American and Caribbean Studies, 1997.

Griffen, William B. *Apaches at War and Peace: The Janos Presidio, 1750–1858*. Tucson: University of Arizona Press, 1979.

———. *Indian Assimilation in the Franciscan Area of Nueva Vizcaya*. Anthropological Papers of the University of Arizona 33. Tucson: University of Arizona Press, 1979.

Griffith, James S. *Beliefs and Holy Places: A Spiritual Geography of the Pimeria Alta*. Tucson: University of Arizona Press, 1992.

Griffiths, Nicholas. Introduction to *Spiritual Encounters: Interactions between Christianity and Native Religions in Colonial America*, edited by Nicholas Griffiths and Fernando Cervantes. Birmingham, UK: University of Birmingham Press, 1999.

Gutiérrez, Ramón A. *When Jesus Came, the Corn Mothers Went Away: Marriage, Sexuality, and Power in New Mexico, 1500–1846*. Stanford, CA: Stanford University Press, 1991.

Guy, Donna J. and Thomas E. Sheridan. "On Frontiers." In *Contested Ground: Comparative Frontiers on the Northern and Southern Edges of the Spanish Empire*, edited by Donna J. Guy and Thomas E. Sheridan, 1–15. Tucson: University of Arizona Press, 1998.

Hall, Thomas D. "The Rio de la Plata and the Greater Southwest." In *Contested Ground: Comparative Frontiers on the Northern and Southern Edges of the Spanish Empire*, edited by Donna J. Guy and Thomas E. Sheridan, 150–66. Tucson: University of Arizona Press, 1998.

———. *Social Change in the Southwest, 1350–1880*. Lawrence: University Press of Kansas, 1989.

Hefner, Robert W. "Introduction: World Building and the Rationality of Conversion." In *Conversion to Christianity: Historical and Anthropological*

Perspectives on a Great Transformation, edited by Robert W. Hefner, 3–44. Berkeley: University of California Press, 1993.

Hoijer, Harry. *Chiricahua and Mescalero Apache Texts with Ethnological Notes by Morris E. Opler*. Chicago: University of Chicago Press, 1938.

Ivey, Jake. "Building Missions." *Bajada: Joining Research and Management* 6, no. 1. U.S. Geological Survey: Cooperative Park Studies Unit at the University of Arizona, 1998.

Jackson, Robert H. *Indian Population Decline: The Missions of Northwestern New Spain, 1687–1840*. Albuquerque: University of New Mexico Press, 1994.

———, ed. *New Views of Borderlands History*. Albuquerque: University of New Mexico Press, 1998.

———. "Northwestern New Spain." In *New Views of Borderlands History*, ed. Robert H. Jackson, 73–97. Albuquerque: University of New Mexico Press, 1998.

John, Elizabeth A. H. *Storms Brewed in Other Men's Worlds: The Confrontation of Indians, Spanish, and French in the Southwest, 1540–1795*. Lincoln: University of Nebraska Press, 1975.

Jones, Oakah L., Jr. *Los Paisanos: Spanish Settlers on the Northern Frontier of New Spain*. Norman: University of Oklahoma Press, 1979.

Karns, Harry J. *Luz de Tierra Incognita: Juan Mateo Manje; Unknown Arizona and Sonora 1693–1701*. Tucson: Arizona Silhouettes, 1954.

Kessell, John L. *Friars, Soldiers, and Reformers: Hispanic Arizona and the Sonora Mission Frontier, 1767–1856*. Tucson: University of Arizona Press, 1976.

———. "Friars versus Bureaucrats: The Mission as a Threatened Institution on the Arizona-Sonora Frontier, 1767–1842." *Western Historical Quarterly* (April 1974): 151–62.

———. *Mission of Sorrows: Jesuit Guevavi and the Pimas, 1691–1767*. Tucson: University of Arizona Press, 1970.

———. *Spain in the Southwest: A Narrative History of Colonial New Mexico, Arizona, Texas, and California*. Norman: University of Oklahoma Press, 2002.

Kidwell, Clara Sue. *Choctaws and Missionaries in Mississippi, 1818–1918*. Norman: University of Oklahoma Press, 1995.

———, Homer Noley, and George E. "Tink" Tinker. *A Native American Theology*. Maryknoll, NY: Orbis Books, 2001.

Lamb, Susan. *Tumacacori: National Historical Park*. Tucson, AZ: Southwest Parks and Monument Association, 1993.

McCarty, Kieran, OFM. *Desert Documentary: The Spanish Years, 1767–1821*. Tucson: Arizona Historical Society, 1976.

———. "Franciscan Beginnings on the Arizona-Sonora Desert, 1767–1770." PhD diss., Catholic University of America, 1973.

———. "Jesuits and Franciscans." In *The Pimería Alta: Missions and More*, edited by James E. Officer, Mardith Scheutz-Miller, and Bernard L. Fontana, 35–45. Tucson: Southwestern Mission Research Center, 1996.

Matson, Daniel S., and Bernard L. Fontana, eds. and trans. *Friar Bringas Reports to the King: Methods of Indoctrination on the Frontier of New Spain 1796–97.* Tucson: University of Arizona Press, 1977.

Miller, Robert Ryal, and William J. Orr, eds. *Daily Life in Colonial Mexico: The Journey of Friar Ilarione de Bergama, 1761–1768.* Translated by William J. Orr. Norman: University of Oklahoma Press, 2000.

Moorhead, Max L. *The Apache Frontier: Jacobo Ugarte and Spanish-Indian Relations in Northern New Spain, 1769–1791.* Norman: University of Oklahoma Press, 1968.

———. *The Presidio: Bastion of the Spanish Borderlands.* Norman: University of Oklahoma Press, 1975.

———. "Spanish Deportation of Hostile Apaches: The Policy and the Practice." *Arizona and the West* 17, no. 3 (1975): 205–20.

Naylor, Thomas H., and Charles W. Polzer, SJ, eds. *The Presidio and Militia on the Northern Frontier of New Spain 1570–1700.* Tucson: University of Arizona Press, 1986.

Nentvig, Juan, SJ. *Rudo Ensayo: A Description of Sonora and Arizona in 1764.* Translated by Alberto Francisco Pradeau and Robert R. Rasmussen. Tucson: University of Arizona Press, 1980.

Och, Joseph, SJ. *Missionary in Sonora: The Travel Reports of Joseph Och, S.J., 1755–1767.* Translated by Theodore Treutlein. San Francisco: California Historical Society, 1965.

Officer, James. *Hispanic Arizona, 1536–1856.* Tucson: University of Arizona Press, 1987.

———, Mardith Scheutz-Miller, and Bernard L. Fontana, eds. *The Pimeria Alta: Missions and More.* Tucson: The Southwestern Mission Research Center, 1996.

Opler, Morris Edward. *Myths and Tales of the Chiricahua Apache Indians.* Lincoln: University of Nebraska Press, 1994.

———. *An Apache Life-Way: The Economic, Social, & Religious Institutions of the Chiricahua Indians.* Lincoln: University of Nebraska Press, 1996.

Park, Joseph F. "Spanish Indian Policy in Northern Mexico, 1765–1810." *Plains Anthropologist* 25, no. 90 (1980): 325–44.

Parsons, Francis B. *Early 17th Century Missions of the Southwest.* Tucson, AZ: Dale Stewart King, 1966.

Perez, Robert Christian. "Indian Rebellions in Northwestern New Spain: A Comparative Analysis, 1695–1750s." PhD diss., University of California, Riverside, 2003.

Perrone, Bobette, H. Henrietta Stockel, and Victoria Krueger. *Medicine Women, Curanderas, and Women Doctors.* Norman: University of Oklahoma Press, 1989.

Perry, Richard J. *Apache Reservation: Indigenous Peoples & the American State.* Austin: University of Texas Press, 1993.

———. "The Apachean Transition from the Subarctic to the Southwest." *Plains Anthropologist* 25, no. 90 (1980): 279–96.

Pfefferkorn, Ignaz. *Sonora: A Description of the Province.* Tucson: University of Arizona Press, 1989.

Pickens, Buford, ed. *The Missions of Northern Sonora: A 1935 Field Documentation.* Tucson: University of Arizona Press, 1993.

Polzer, Charles William, SJ. "The Evolution of the Jesuit Mission System in Northern New Spain, 1600–1767." PhD diss., University of California, Riverside, 1972.

———, ed. "The Franciscan Entrada into Sonora, 1645–1652. A Jesuit Chronicle." *Arizona and the West* 14, no. 3 (1972): 253–78.

———. *Kino: A Legacy.* Tucson: Jesuit Fathers of Arizona, 1998.

———. "Kino in Mexico." Lecture, Sierra Lutheran Church, Sierra Vista, AZ, February 14, 2001.

———. *Rules and Precepts of the Jesuit Missions of Northwestern New Spain.* Tucson: University of Arizona Press, 1976.

Radding, Cynthia. "The Común, Local Governance, and Defiance in Colonial Sonora." In *Choice, Persuasion, and Coercion: Social Control on Spain's North American Frontiers*, edited by Jesús F. de la Teja and Ross Frank, 179–99. Albuquerque: University of New Mexico Press, 2005.

Reff, Daniel T. "Critical Introduction." In *History of the Triumphs of our Holy Faith Amongst the Most Barbarous and Fierce Peoples of the New World*, by Andrés Pérez de Ribas, 11–46. Translated by Daniel T. Reff, Maureen Ahearn, and Richard K. Danford. Annotated by Daniel T. Reff. Tucson: University of Arizona Press, 1999.

———. *Diseases, Depopulation and Culture Change in Northwestern New Spain, 1518–1764.* Salt Lake City: University of Utah Press, 1991.

Ricard, Robert. *The Spiritual Conquest of Mexico.* Translated by Lesley Byrd Simpson. Berkeley: University of California Press, 1966.

Salmón, Roberto Mario. *Indian Revolts in Northern New Spain: A Synthesis of Resistance.* Lanham, MD: University Press of America, 1991.

Salpointe, Most Rev. J. B., DD. *Soldiers of the Cross: Notes on the Ecclesiastical History of New Mexico, Arizona, and Colorado.* Banning, CA: St. Boniface's Industrial School, 1898.

Santiago, Mark. *The Red Captain: The Life of Hugo O'Conor Commandant Inspector of the Interior Provinces of New Spain.* Museum Monograph 9. Tucson: Arizona Historical Society, 1994.

Sauer, Carl. *Aboriginal Population of Northwestern Mexico.* Berkeley: University of California Press, 1935.

———. *The Road to Cibola.* Berkeley: University of California Press, 1932.

Schweinfurth, Kay Parker. *Prayer on Top of the Earth: The Spiritual Universe of the Plains Indians*. Boulder: University Press of Colorado, 2002.

Seymour, Deni J. "The Implications of Mobility, Reoccupation, and Low Visibility Phenomena for Chronometric Dating." Unpublished paper, 2006–7.

Sheridan, Cecelia. "Social Control and Native Territoriality in Northeastern New Spain." In *Choice, Persuasion, and Coercion: Social Control on Spain's North American Frontiers*, edited by Jesús F. de la Teja and Ross Frank, 121–48. Albuquerque: University of New Mexico Press, 2005.

Simpson, Lesley Byrd. *The Encomienda in New Spain: The Beginning of Spanish Mexico*. Berkeley: University of California Press, 1950.

Smith, Fay Jackson, John L. Kessell, and Francis J. Fox, SJ. *Father Kino in Arizona*. Phoenix: Arizona Historical Foundation, 1966.

Spicer, Edward H. *Cycles of Conquest: The Impact of Spain, Mexico, and the United States on Indians of the Southwest, 1533–1960*. Tucson: University of Arizona Press, 1962.

Stern, Peter. "Marginals and Acculturation in Frontier Society." In *New Views of Borderlands History*, edited by Robert H. Jackson, 157–88. Albuquerque: University of New Mexico Press, 1998.

——. "Social Marginality and Acculturation on the Northern Frontier of New Spain." PhD diss., University of California, Berkeley, 1984.

Stockel, H. Henrietta. *On the Bloody Road to Jesus: Christianity and the Chiricahua Apaches*. Albuquerque: University of New Mexico Press, 2004.

——. *Chiricahua Apache Women and Children: Safekeepers of the Heritage*. College Station: Texas A & M University Press, 2000.

——. *Survival of the Spirit: Chiricahua Apaches in Captivity*. Reno: University of Nevada Press, 1993.

——. *Women of the Apache Nation: Voices of Truth*. Reno: University of Nevada Press, 1991.

Sweeney, Edwin R. *Cochise: Chiricahua Apache Chief*. Norman: University of Oklahoma Press, 1991.

Sweet, David. "The Ibero-American Frontier Mission in Native American History." In *The New Latin American Mission History*, edited by Eric Langer and Robert H. Jackson, 1–48. Lincoln: University of Nebraska Press, 1995.

Teja, Jesús F. de la, and Ross Frank, eds. *Choice, Persuasion, and Coercion: Social Control on Spain's North American Frontiers*. Albuquerque: University of New Mexico Press, 2005.

Treutlein, Theodore E. "The Economic Regime of the Jesuit Missions in Eighteenth Century Sonora." *Pacific Historical Review* 8 (1939): 289–300.

"Tumacacori Historic High Mass." U.S. Department of the Interior, National Park Service, 1999.

Vecsey, Christopher. *On the Padres' Trail*. Notre Dame, IN: University of Notre Dame Press, 1996.

Weber, David J. *The Spanish Frontier in North America*. New Haven, CT: Yale University Press, 1992.

West, Robert C. *Sonora: Its Geographical Personality*. Austin: University of Texas Press, 1993.

Whiting, Alfred F., ed. "The Tumacacori Census of 1796." *The Kiva* 19 (1953): 1–12.

Williams, Lyle W. "Struggle for Survival: The Hostile Frontier of New Spain, 1750–1800." PhD diss., Texas Christian University, 1970.

Wormser, Richard. *Tubac*. Tubac, AZ: Tubac Historical Society, 1975.

Zavala, Silvio. "The Frontiers of Hispanic America." In *New Spain's Far Northern Frontier: Essays on Spain in the American West 1540–1821*, edited by David J. Weber, 179–99. Albuquerque: University of New Mexico Press, 1979.

Index

Page numbers in italic text indicate illustrations.

Clemente, Gaspar, OFM, 101; baptizes Apache slaves at Tumacácori, 121
Cochise, 9, 12
Coppersmith, Clifford, 6
Cruikshank, Julia, 6, 144n3
Cuba, 5, 70–110, 142; Apache prisoners escape, refuse alliance, 136; crown approves deportation of Apaches, 109; destination of Apache slaves, 70–110; ethnogenesis, 134; plan for Apache slave distribution, 109; receives prisoners, 136
Cutter, Donald, 38

Deloria, Vine, Jr.: deficient Bering Strait theory, 2
diseases: among Anza's troops, 76; Apache prisoners' death from, 136; chronic, 67–68, 152n1; contagious, 54; epidemics, 54, 67–68, 150n65; ghost sickness, 19; indigenes' vulnerability to, 67; smallpox, 136; syphilis, 102–4
Dobyns, Henry, 70–110

earth: Apaches, sustenance, 11–12; moral significance to indigenes, 11; sacred, 11
Eixarch, Tomás, OFM, 102
encomienda, 113–14
Englehardt, Zephyrin, OFM, 66
Engstrand, Iris, 38
ethnogenesis: as Apache characteristic, 144n8; definition of, 8; during migration, 128; missions aid, 134
eurocentrism, 28; cultural supremacy of, 1; disdain, 132; incoming Spaniards' practice, 2; proof of superiority, 30; responsible for cultural collision, 4; underlying premise of, 30

Farrer, Claire R., 6, 144n1
Faulk, Odie B., 94
Font, Pedro, OFM, 51
Fontana, Bernard, 58
Forbes, Jack D.: describes Athapaskan migrations, 7
Franciscans, 57–69, *103*, 142; ailing, 67–68; annual stipend, 59; Arriquibar, 102; assigned to northern Mexico, 3, 58; biological possibilities, 152n88; Bordoy, 105; Buena y Alcalde describes missions, 58; Carillo, 80; characteristics, 133; Clemente, 60; Eixarch, 102; Englehardt, 66; Font, 51; forced labor, 65, 101; Garces, 62; García, 64; Garrucho, 119; Gil de Bernabé, 60; goals, 3, 5; guidelines limit their control, 59; Guillén, 64; guilty of genocide, 137; Gutiérrez, 80, 104; instructions, 59; Janos, 105; language barrier, 65; López, 105; McCarty, 7, 69; Moreno, 102; prohibitions, missions, 59; Roche, 65; Salazar, 128; Salpointe, 58; sell Apache children, 105, 121–26; sell Apache men and women, 116; trafficking in human slavery, 4; Ximeno, 60; Zúñiga, 60. *See also* individual names
Frank, Ross: violation of celibacy, 103

Gálvez, Bernardo de: Instructions of 1786, 68; Viceroy of New Spain, 68
Gálvez, José de, 142; emissary to Carlos III, 94; recommendations, 94
Garate, Don: describes indigenes at Calabazas, 62; important quote, 62

Gálvez, Bernardo de, 68; intensified military campaigns, 104; objectives, 68–69

Jackson, Robert, 42
Janos, 5, 70–110, *107–8*, 141; Apache attacks, 106, 108; Apache women, 106; Apaches arrive, 106; Apaches' attitude toward Christianity, 130; encounters with Apaches, 106; Franciscans, 105; mission, 70–110; names of Apache leaders, 108; names of children sold by priests, 125–26; overcrowded, 105; population, 109; population of Apaches, 108–9; presidio, 70–110
Januske, Daniel, SJ, 51
Jesuits, 37–57, 141–42; Aguirre, 100; annual stipend, 30; assignment, 30; Bible, Genesis permits Christian dominion, 42; biological possibility, 152n88; Campos, 48; characteristics, 38, 133; Christianity gives permission to indoctrinate indigenes, 37; Company of Jesuits founded, 29; courage, 41; daily routine, 57; duties, 30, 37; egocentrism, 30; Espinosa, 50; expulsion from northern Mexico, 55–56; García de Noriega, 126; Garrucho, 48; Grazhoffer, 48; goals, 3–5; guilty of genocide, 137; Januske, 52; Keller, 40; Kino appears, 38; language barrier, 45; Montaño, 126; names of children sold, 118–26; Navarrete, 125; Nentvig, 52; Nieto, 125; Och, 57; papal bull of 1546, 37; Pauer, 48; Perera, 46; Pérez de Ribas, Provincial, 41; Pineli, 50; Polzer explains *reducción/congregación*, 31–32;

Ponce de León, 125; purpose, 30; Rapicani, 88; risk retaliation, 149n43; San Martín, 48; Sedelmayr, 52; Segesser, 38; sell Apaches, 116; Stiger, 50; teach indigenes, 54; Torres Perea, 88; trafficking in human slavery, 4; Tubutama as general headquarters, 51; Ures, 38; Vivas, 52. *See also* Bible; individual names
John, Elizabeth A. H.: Apache captives, families, 112
Jones, Oakah L., Jr., 42

Kanseah, Kathleen, 81
Karns, Harry J.: map, *33*
Keller, Ignacio Xavier, SJ: administers Guévavi, 48, 118–19; assignment disappoints, 40; baptizes Pimas, 66; baptizes Apache slaves at San Ignacio, 124; supervises rebuilding Suamca, 53
Kidwell, Clara Sue, 4; describes effect of missions, 42; explains traditions, 11
Kino, Eusebio, SJ, *39*, 141; appears in 1687, 38; celebrates mass at Suamca, 53; death of, 38; founds Tubutama, 51; Manje as military companion, 53; teaches Pimas, 49; first visit to Tubac, 71; visits Guévavi, 46; visits San Ignacio de Cabórica, 50; visits San Xavier del Bac, 49

Laws of the Indies, New, 1542: articles, 115; controversy, 159n17; declarations about indigenes, 32; definition, 141; priests ignore, 45; prohibitions, 45; resistance, 115
López, Rámon, OFM, 105
Los Santos Ángeles de Guévavi. *See also* Guévavi